D0526812

# What's New in Church Leadership?

Malcolm Grundy is the Director of the Foundation for Church Leadership, launched in 2005 by Archbishop Rowan Williams, and dedicated to encouraging and inspiring church leaders as they tackle new challenges in leadership.

He is the author of *What They Don't Teach You at Theological College*, and lives in York.

Also by the same author and available from
Canterbury Press

*What They Don't Teach You at Theological College*

www.canterburypress.co.uk

# What's New in Church Leadership?

*Creative Responses to the Changing Pattern of Church Life*

## Malcolm Grundy

CANTERBURY
PRESS
Norwich

© Malcolm Grundy 2007

First published in 2007 by the Canterbury Press Norwich
(a publishing imprint of Hymns Ancient & Modern Limited,
a registered charity)
9–17 St Alban's Place, London N1 0NX

www.scm-canterburypress.co.uk

All rights reserved. No part of this publication may be reproduced,
stored in a retrieval system, or transmitted,
in any form or by any means, electronic, mechanical,
photocopying or otherwise, without the prior permission of
the publisher, Canterbury Press.

The Author has asserted his right under the Copyright, Designs and
Patents Act, 1988, to be identified as the Author of this Work

British Library Cataloguing in Publication data

A catalogue record for this book is available
from the British Library

ISBN 978-1-85311-799-2

Typeset by Regent Typesetting, London
Printed and bound in Great Britain by
William Clowes Ltd, Beccles, Suffolk

# Contents

For the

Revd Julian Cummins, 1955–2007,

who would have shared all the hopes in this book.

# Foreword

## by Steven Croft

In 2004 I was granted a term's sabbatical by St John's College, Durham and looked more closely at the study of leadership. The study was partly funded by the Foundation for Church Leadership of which Malcolm Grundy is now Director.

During the course of the term I was guided through the literature on leadership by a number of colleagues in the Durham Business School. I made a particular study of the public sector leadership institutions which have flourished over the last decade. I engaged in a more deliberate way with the significant Christian tradition on leadership both in the Bible and in different periods of church history.

I reached the end of the term impressed by the wide range of current thinking on leadership in many different fields and by its congruence with much of the Christian tradition. I was also more convinced than ever of the importance of reflection on leadership within the churches in dialogue both with our Christian heritage and with developments in leadership in our wider society. Just as my sabbatical ended, I was invited to take up my present post. The need for clear thinking about leadership has become, if anything, more important still as I have sought to encourage and reflect on the development of many different fresh expressions of church across the United Kingdom.

Malcolm Grundy offers in this book an accessible, thought-provoking and immensely helpful guide to what is a large and growing field of literature and wisdom. Malcolm brings significant expertise in reflection on leadership within and outside the churches. Over the years I have learned always to listen to what he says with care and attention. He has a thorough grasp of the riches of the Christian faith and tradition and has distilled over many years the insights of practice and research in leadership in a variety of fields.

This book therefore provides a unique introduction to the subject of church leadership; a map to explore different areas in depth and a practical guide to keep beside you when thinking through questions of teamwork, review, consultancy or change. I commend it most warmly.

*The Revd Dr Steven Croft*
*Archbishops' Missioner and Team Leader of Fresh Expressions*

# Preface

Everything and nothing is new in shapes of leadership in today's churches. Everything is new because once familiar situations are adapting, changing or being brought to an end in different ways, by new leaders. Nothing is new in that methods and systems which are emerging as fitting for today can be found in different forms and working well for other situations in previous ages.

This book takes the approach that almost everything is new in the understanding and application of leadership for our churches, and that working together in teams will be an important new way forward. I really do believe that we face previously unexplored situations in local congregations and in our national churches. The challenges of our situation in the United Kingdom can be replicated in many countries elsewhere. Some leadership dilemmas are common to churches across the world. The ways in which we might approach them by using new methods of co-operation and of leadership in multi-talented teams are the substance of this book.

The situations which face local and national church leaders are direct and easy to describe.

- There is a growing interest in spirituality and religious practice after decades of secularization, which were thought to erode belief and the practice of religion.
- There is a decline of regular attendance in most congregations, whose core membership is ageing.
- There is an increase in occasional attendance for special occasions and at some festivals.
- There are fewer stipendiary clergy than for many generations.

# What's New in Church Leadership?

- Almost no one is offering themselves for the Religious Life.
- The need to work in partnership with leaders of other faith communities is now very important.
- There is a decline in the attitude of many people to denominational allegiance.
- New 'shapes' of local church worship are emerging, some only loosely connected to traditional congregations.
- More statistical and research evidence about religious change exists than ever before.
- There is a greater internal and external imperative for clergy and senior leaders to work together in teams.
- The high cost of maintaining traditional forms of church is causing great concern.
- The place of active lay people in the governance of churches is becoming even more significant.
- The overall unity of the world-wide Christian Church is being threatened by a new range of controversies.

These emerging issues bring new challenges to leaders as to members and can be a cause of anxiety and concern. However, these complex situations will give a sense of challenge and excitement to the kind of leadership we need to support and develop for the future. It is that same infectious sense of excitement which has given me energy as I have explored what can and needs to be new in leadership across our denominations.

I am enormously grateful to my friends and colleagues as I have explored new and old understandings of leadership. Christine Smith of SCM-Canterbury Press has been encouraging and supportive throughout. My new associates who run leadership foundations for other professions have shared their knowledge and experience with me in very open ways as have those who offer training and support for senior leaders. Many colleagues will recognize their own ideas and words here. I hope that I have not misrepresented them too much. I have also varied a convention about the use of the word 'church'. As in common usage and to emphasize the context I have not always stuck to Church and church. I have sometimes used church when what is really meant is congregation and sometimes I have said denomination to make a more universal point. I hope that this is more helpful than confusing.

Colleagues in the Church of Sweden have kept me well informed of developments in church life in northern Europe and have given me generous hospitality to work on the revisions of my chapters in lakeside summer houses in their beautiful country. There is no doubt that my greatest thanks have to go to the Trustees of the Foundation for Church Leadership for appointing me as their first director. This new post has placed me in a large room at a most appropriate time in my own ministry and professional development. This book contains my own ideas and work and does not reflect the views of my Trustees or of FCL. Many new colleagues in other walks of life have helped me to see that the contribution of the churches to their work is welcome and valued. The opportunities for the denominations to share their experiences of leadership and to learn from others are more available than ever before. I have been welcomed into very privileged places in what has become a formative time in my own life. I hope that my discoveries and reflections will give at least an introduction to much that is new in leadership and that those who need to explore more will find my promptings and avenues provocative and enticing.

*Malcolm Grundy*
*Michaelmas 2006*

# New Foundations for Church Leadership

Leading today's Church is tough. A predominantly secular, sometimes hostile culture, the challenge of relating to other faiths, declining numbers of worshippers and resources, internal church disputes, the need to foster fresh expressions of being church – all these add to the challenges of leading what is still a large and primarily voluntary organization. Church leaders face a myriad of demands from the members they also serve. They are often inadequately trained to do so and are always under-resourced.

The effectiveness of any organization depends, in large part, on the quality of its leaders. The Church is no different in this respect. If it is to be an effective instrument of God's mission on earth, it needs leaders who can inspire and persuade others to share its vision of love and action in the world.

Good leadership is full of humanity, experience, wisdom, energy and pragmatism. Those who become leaders wear the scars of injury and defeat as well as the medals and rewards earned by perseverance and achievement. Looking back on his time as President of the USA, Lyndon Johnson mused: 'The presidency makes the very man who occupies it, no matter how small, bigger than he was, and no matter how big, not big enough for its demands.' Women and men who have become leaders know that to be true. In order to reflect in this way any leader will have shown some promise, had the confidence to face a range of tasks and, in all likelihood, ended up with a feeling that they might have done better.

In a time of increasing openness to spirituality, Christianity faces enormous opportunities, which can only be taken up if churches are well led. Church leaders have to be extremely alert both to where growth can take place and also to where misplaced activity will waste energy. The development of new ways of leading our churches will provide the keys to open doors to new understandings of Christianity and to the creation of structures which enable growth to be consolidated. Leadership is much more than a fashionable word. It is at the heart of what makes each one of us feel optimistic about our faith and about belonging to a church.

Some leadership issues apply only to churches, but most are common to all organizations working in a world of change, tension and opportunity. Members of congregations are learning one elementary truth – in order to survive, local congregations and national churches need to continue to evolve. They will be different from the ones which shaped us and which many of us know and cherish today.

What's new in leadership is that it needs to be seen and valued in every part of life. What's new in *church* leadership is that a word once so suspect has now become a way of understanding the life and work of Jesus. He called and led his disciples in a particular way; and how he ordered his own life, with its joys, triumphs, frustrations and sacrifices, is one of the world's great examples of leadership self-awareness. From its earliest days the Church has been seen as the Body of Christ on earth, and as such its continuation of Jesus' sacrificial, servant-leadership is a concept which seems to have come of age.

## Leaders and leadership

Some leaders are made by circumstances, while others seem to be born with a gene which drives and shapes them. One of life's eternal dilemmas is determining exactly what kind of environment produces a leader. Undoubtedly the history of any developed country contains stories of those who were born 'with a silver spoon in their mouth', and who took to leadership as their birthright. Equally there are those potential leaders who had birth, education and wealth on their side, but were unable to rise to the challenge. Many more lacked a good start in life but against all odds became great leaders. There are those who have led through influence and example and are regarded as leaders even though they never held high office. Many rise to positions of importance through making the very most of a spark within themselves which wants to achieve and be fulfilled. Some have much asked of them and realize the potential others saw in them. There is no need for leadership to be seen as the habitation of unbridled ambition.

There are other 'great' leaders who took people to misplaced ends. History is littered with examples of destructive leadership, and for our purposes Hitler and Mussolini will do. Our detailed examination will show what an elusive attainment good leadership is, even though it is one for which far more people could be equipped.

Good church leadership is not seen and experienced everywhere. Leaders vary in ability and talent, as well as in experience or intellect. They have reached their seniority in many and varied ways. History says that some elected or appointed to senior positions were not equipped for the task, however much the consoling thoughts of a Lyndon Johnson might think the office enlarges its holder. Those who get to be leaders know that their success has depended to some degree on chance and on being in the right place at the right time. Their experience and intuition helped them make sure that circumstances pointed their way. Other equally suitable but unappointed candidates see life as a lottery and themselves as unfortunate victims. Some who have built a career on personal achievement and ambition still lack the qualities which engage followers' active commitment or support. Others have ability which is not recognized either through their own timidity or because less able but more 'streetwise' people have learned to push themselves forward. Irrespective of appropriate ability, others are appointed for partisan or political reasons. Many in our churches, as in all walks of life, have the potential to become influential leaders if their contribution is recognized and developed. One of the tragedies of any organization is that such people gradually cease to give of their best through lack of support and affirmation long before their working lives are ended.

## The bigger picture

Before we rush into looking at work inside the churches it is important to remember that leadership is exercised by Christians in almost every aspect of life. While it would be a mistake to write about Christian leadership as only being exercised in the churches, or rather the denominations, this book will take leadership within those denominations as its main focus. It is where this author has spent most of his life, while giving many years to supporting those who are exposed in other ways to questions and responsibilities in leadership throughout industry, commerce, the caring professions and the voluntary sector. What will be unfolded in subsequent chapters comes from a variety of sources, many from places where Christians have been influential in the 'secular' world. It can be applied very appropriately to our churches.

Sharing experience about leadership has to be a two-way process. Clearly, there are values and beliefs of Christians and those of other faiths which influence the way in which societies operate and in which business is done. I was once Chair of MODEM, an 'at the edge' leadership organization trying to encourage an exchange of experience between leaders in Christian churches and those in other places. It worked well and our three books on management and leadership became, in church terms, best sellers. Most of the contributors to all three books were not church leaders recognized by the senior appointments system but were committed to improving leadership in their own churches. Their contributions demonstrated that Christian leadership is exercised in many places in the churches and far beyond.

Mature leadership within a denomination is not threatened or challenged by new ideas. Many different forms of leadership have to be experienced and then gradually reflected in a changing church as appointments systems themselves adapt to different profiles and demands. Christianity can bring inventiveness, a strong sense of values and a critique to leadership, good and bad, but it cannot hijack the whole territory. Learning about how to develop partnerships will be one of the essential characteristics of leadership in churches that are adapting to change. Beliefs and values are the hub from which all life and change will radiate. They inform every area of life in which church people exercise influence and leadership.

## A new context

New questions have arisen in today's churches, which require special kinds of leadership to resolve. They stem from the enormous changes which have taken place in society affecting the way in which faith and organized religion are understood. The profile of congregations has changed, as has the supply of ministers. Congregations are now paying more than ever for their clergy and will not sit back and uncritically accept what they are given. We now know more than ever before about how congregations grow and why some decline. Research backs up what many would regard as self-evident – that old and new members respond to the individual qualities of pastoral care, preaching and leadership of their minister. Congregations grow because the gifts of everyone are utilized to their fullest effect and affirmation becomes mutual. In 2004 Dr Keith Wulff, head of the Research Office of the Presbyterian Churches in the USA, conducted a survey of US Presbyterian churches, which were growing. Volumes of number crunching research concluded three simple factors about congregations which flourish with their own minister:

1 The minister was able to articulate a strong and credible vision which they were seen to live out in their own beliefs and actions.
2 Congregation members were willing to invite others to join.
3 The minister was willing to share leadership responsibilities with members.

Of course there are historical and cultural differences either side of the Atlantic. From the US ideal of the sensitive pastor to which a community will respond a new pattern of churchgoing is emerging in the UK and in many parts of Europe. While fewer people than for centuries go to church week by week, more people than for decades are willing to consider the possibility of a spiritual dimension in their life. The challenge for churches is to convert new patterns of attendance into deeper commitment – and with fewer full-time paid ministers. Doors swing open at times of national mourning or celebration and at main Christian and national festivals. At Christmas in 2004 it was predicted that 43% of the adult population of England was likely to attend church. The organization Christian Research has provided statistics about church attendance for many years (www.christian-research.org.uk). In their book *Religious Trends 2005/6* they begin by telling us the rather well-known fact that in the 2001 National Census 72% of those living in the UK said they were Christian. A little later they supply a graph showing a peak of clergy retiring early in their mid-50s, ten years before the normal retirement age. Questions of morale, affirmation and appropriate leadership support leap from the page.

The move from occasional attendance to committed membership cannot be achieved without properly trained and equipped leaders – clergy and lay. Those who believe only in a static form of church or in the retrenchment associated with decline will not develop the skills and experience to lead a renewed church. At the risk of alienating some readers for the rest of this book I suggest a military example is appropriate. When General Bernard Montgomery took over command of the Eighth Army in North Africa, he discovered that all the plans they were making were for positions of retreat and retrenchment. He turned attitudes around, communicating to people at all levels that plans from then on were about how and where to advance.

The right choice of present and future church leaders is vital. They need that kind of strategic forward-looking vision. It is the only way our church members can have confidence in their future within a denomination. I am convinced that our next generation of leaders will not be effective working alone. Different types of available staff, some lay and some ordained, some with pastoral and administrative gifts and some with specialisms, mean that leadership is a matter of forming and developing teams. Sensitive, self-aware leaders will not appoint insubstantial or like-minded people. They will look for those with the right range of skills to complement one another. Together, they will build and share a vision of what they want to achieve.

## Starting from here

The scale of change is clear and a different pattern of church life is emerging. The numbers of full-time paid ministers in all the historic denominations continues to decline, as also does the number of those who attend regularly – that is weekly, fortnightly or monthly. Each denomination seems to record and present its figures in a slightly different way. The Church of England saw a reduction of 6% in its stipendiary ministers between 2000 and 2004. It began 2005 with 8,897 in comparison with an estimated 24,500 in 1900. The statistics for the Methodist Church show a decline in membership of 9.7% between 2001 and 2004. The number of Roman Catholic clergy has reduced from 4,755 in 1981 to 3,765 in 2003. Those in the Religious Life in England and Wales went from 2,266 to 1,363 in the same period. There is an increase in people who are ordained but not paid or who carry out authorized lay roles in the denominations. In the Roman Catholic Church there is an increase in those entering the diaconate. In the Baptist Church in England and South Wales (The Baptist Union) there were 132,440 members in 2000 and in 2004 there were 118,022. In 2000 there were 1,709 Pastors in Charge, paid and unpaid, and in 2004 the number rose to 1,911. Again, Christian Research have produced the most comprehensive profile of churchgoing in English churches.[1] It has the most captivating title – *Pulling Out of the Nosedive* – and demonstrates a slowing in the decline of those attending church together with astonishing facts of many kinds, especially about the places where young people are attending churches.

The number of church buildings has reduced but not on the same scale as the number of ministers and church members. It is estimated that across the denominations in Great Britain two church buildings close each week. There were 37,500 churches in England in May 2005. Over two-fifths (43%) of these were Anglican and almost a further fifth (16%) were Methodist. All the other denominations make up the remaining two-fifths or 41%. The denominations which saw the most growth were the independent churches, the Pentecostal and Free Evangelical churches, all of which have benefited from the explosive growth of black majority churches and those of other ethnic origins. The denomination which closed the most churches was the Methodist Church following a programme of rationalization. One quarter of its listed building chapels have a registered membership of 15 or less. New partnerships are likely to find different and creative uses for many of these buildings.

Many of these valuable church buildings are part of the national heritage and need to be conserved in some appropriate way. Some of those deprived of the possibility of worshipping in their local church develop new ways to meet, sometimes with and sometimes without the active support of their local minister. The challenge is not to spread traditional coverage even more thinly but to understand the situation and then to develop and appoint leaders who can take churches and congregations on to new ways of developing a vibrant local life – with the best kind of buildings.

## New questions to explore

There are those asking more radical questions and wondering if the different understandings of congregational life and the leadership role of the ordained minister are able to be contained within the same understanding of Church. Are the changing shapes and expressions of local churches compatible with received traditions and historical understandings of ministry? Are the divisions over interpretations of the Bible and who can and who cannot minister in an official capacity to a congregation so deep that a denomination is no longer a common community of faith and practice? In the local church there are those who wonder if one congregation and one minister or ministerial team can sustain and lead significantly different congregations. Some ministers and church members wonder how much they have in common with the senior leadership and values of their denomination.

In the language of church life and growth there have emerged two helpful, though over simplified, terms to describe what is happening. To explore adaptation and development in churches as they have been experienced for the last century or longer there is often talk about how to manage the *inherited church*. In contrast, when talking about new patterns of worship and congregational life which have not developed from the adaptation of a previous model or structure, we have now come to talk about the *emerging church*. Research into these new forms is being conducted in a programme called Fresh Expressions led by Steve Croft with a team of Anglican and Methodist colleagues. The work is described in a series of stimulating publications and an interactive website, www.freshexpressions.com.uk.

In an inherited church, which is where most churchgoers find themselves, what patterns of leadership are needed now and for the foreseeable future? If more congregations are to be grouped together, as they surely are, what else has to change? What will bring about a different expectation from that of everyone having their own minister, who is available for them at all times? What will happen to clergy who come in with that understanding of their job and live a life of frustration? What will be the characteristics of an emerging church? Many hope that a new kind of leadership will take hold of these questions and develop a vision of mutual responsibility where congregations feel part of a 'family' in a locality and where those called to different types of leadership – administrator, pastor, teacher, preacher, prayer leader – will be valued and trained according to their particular gifts.

## A personal story

When we arrived in York in the spring of 2005 my wife and I began to attach ourselves to a delightful community-based church where the parish communion is the weekly norm. Our excellent vicar had another parish and other city-centre responsibilities. In our irregular attendance over several months we saw worship led on some occasions by a visiting celebrant and preacher and on others by a retired or specialist minister. Perhaps we had just been on 'the wrong weeks' or perhaps we were experiencing the same thing as many other people. Our vicar presided twice and we did not hear him preach. This is some new-shape church! We were kept there by the quality of the worship and through the well-organized ministries of a considerable group of lay people. It is quite obvious that it is the weekday pastoral, social and organizational effectiveness of the minister and team which makes this church work. There was no dependency on the personality and pull of the minister. If there were some who hankered after past days and a different ministerial style there was no evidence that a previous pattern had produced a larger or healthier congregation. My many years as an archdeacon taught me that if any congregation was asked what they wanted they would say that they wanted their own vicar. My experience was also that where ministerial teams were formed and ministry was shared, even with fewer ministers, the vitality of local congregations was increased.

Planning for an advance rather than for a retreat will require confidence in a new picture of a church led in different ways. Underneath this will be a firm conviction that God is calling the Church to develop different forms in different places. Shared leadership will not be a reinvention of a Methodist Circuit system or an adaptation of the large Roman Catholic parish, or even a rediscovery of life as it might have been in the Early Church. It will be a new form which will have as its bedrock a shared understanding of how churches and congregations are led. It cannot be one burdened by too many roles and tasks focused on the person who wears the clerical collar.

## A ministry of oversight

A new and rather technical word is emerging to encompass concepts of shared ministry and the place of the ordained. The word
*episcope* used to be linked primarily with the work and responsibilities of bishops. It means *oversight* and is coming to be used to
describe the care of a group or series of congregations. It is now
described as the kind of responsibility to which many stipendiary
ministers will be called. If such a transfer of responsibility, and
even of power, is taking place big changes are afoot in our
churches. If episcope is taken away from the bishop, the principal
focus of ministry in episcopally led denominations, are we undo-
ing nearly 2,000 years of church order? This is unlikely but it
could signify a shift in understandings of the way in which both
oversight and authority are exercised. Bishops themselves could
feel liberated from unrealistic expectations and supported in new
ways by clergy and congregations. They could rediscover the
potential in their teaching, liturgical and representative roles.
It would be good if these conceptual changes did take away
inherited ideas of hierarchy and the privileges which go with
them once and for all but that is unlikely. Most of those in non-
episcopal churches would admit they are equally familiar with
the weight of top-down structures.

It all starts at the grass-roots. Leaders can only come from
existing congregations, of whatever kind. It will always be the
selection and development processes that are important. Some
candidates will still feel an individual sense of call and offer themselves for full-time ministerial and priestly work within the
church. Others, perhaps more than in the past, will have the idea
suggested to them from recognition by those who know them
and who can see what they would have to offer in a new role.
Ideas about the practical outworking of ministry come from the
experience and receipt of good work from previous generations
of ministers who 'model' what can be thought of as an inspirational ideal. What may very well now be needed is a revision of
that model if ideas about vocation to a ministry of oversight and
team leadership are to play a significant part in their work.

## The development of new leaders

It is the selection and development track that is important in the identification of skills and abilities for future senior leaders. Examples from biographies and stories of heroes frequently show that they were 'spotted' by a good teacher or patron who educated and groomed them. An environment in which it is possible for promising people to rise in an organization is one where a greater number are likely to be encouraged to give of their best.

From the time of the first appointment leadership skills can be identified and developed. The newness begins here because we need to see our churches or denominations as a whole and not as a series of separate units. Those who recommend and those who select need to look for a different kind of person who will develop into someone who will help create and lead a different kind of church (Figure 1). Some will have great titles and large organiza-

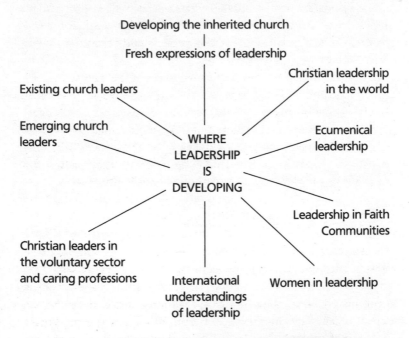

Figure 1: Developing leadership in today's churches

tional responsibilities. Others will lead and bring about change from the edges.

## FOUR FOUNDATION STONES FOR CHRISTIAN LEADERSHIP

In order to establish sustainable new patterns of leadership I offer four foundation stones on which firm new understandings of leadership can be built. These are:

- a developing sense of vocation
- asking who Jesus Christ is for us today
- a search for the tasks we are called to perform
- a strategic approach to leadership

When each of these is explored in a lifetime of learning then a balance is reached and secure understandings of Christian leadership emerge. Some trainers and spiritual advisers use the word '*formation*' to describe this lifelong process and I consider myself one of them.

We never arrive at the person we want to be and we rarely achieve the understandings of our work that we would like. Each development produces a new set of ideas and challenges. Consequently a continuing sense of exploration is necessary for a Christian leader to be effective. Many of those who take this journey say that the one constant ingredient in their search for meaning and fulfilment is the need to remain inquisitive!

### I A developing sense of vocation

If it is accurate to say that congregational life is becoming more local, reflecting different approaches to ministry, this raises issues about the nature of vocation. What kind of church are ministers being called into? What do congregations and denominations expect when they call their ministers? What can society expect in terms of spiritual leadership from those who lead local congregations – or regional parts of national denominations? Such enormous questions run through understandings of the structure and practice of religion. They connect with our beliefs about how Christian people should form community and they pose fundamental and stimulating challenges to those who exercise leadership in our churches.

The word 'vocation' has its roots in the idea of being called to a particular work and style of life. It comes from the Latin word *vocare* which means to call. There is a sense in which vocation has been taken over by the caring professions and by the churches but its meaning is wider and not confined to a personal journey or work in a particular profession. For me, living a fulfilled vocation has come to be linked to the idea of living all of life in a responsive way. I have come to this understanding through years of being fed by the writings of the German pastor and martyr Dietrich Bonhoeffer. From his Lutheran background and tradition he came to reflect on this understanding of vocation or 'calling'.

> In the encounter with Jesus Christ (man) hears the call of God and in it the calling to life in the fellowship of Jesus Christ . . . Now a man takes up his position against the world *in* the world; the calling is the place at which the call of God is answered, the place at which a man lives responsibly.[2]

Bonhoeffer looked at Martin Luther's contrast between the responsibilities of his former monastic life and those he took on when he chose to live in the outside world. He spoke of a 'yes' to God when a decision is made in obedience to follow Christ and a 'no' to the world as it is experienced. The responsibility of living in the world is full of compromises. In an inspired connection with the purpose of Christ's death and resurrection Bonhoeffer sees the human 'yes' to working out a vocation in the world as collaborating with God's 'yes' in Christ through which he is reconciling the world to himself. A living sense of vocation has to be one which changes and develops as tasks and responsibilities change. This is as true within the Church as anywhere else. In no other way can a Christian experience a ministry which continues to have energy and vitality.

## 2 Asking who Jesus Christ is for us today

When Bonhoeffer was training his students in a seminary under a growing Nazi regime he gave them one significant piece of advice – to keep on asking, in each generation, how the person and ministry of Jesus Christ should be understood and interpreted.

The question was fundamental to his thought and teaching. He began, according to accounts of his teaching in 1933 recorded by Ebehard Bethge, by asking 'How has Christ been understood and what is wrong with classical concepts of Christology?' He looks again and again in the developing events of his life for new understandings of Christ. In his book *Christology*, first published in Britain in 1966,[3] he describes how Christ is known through the silent reflections on his person in the spirituality of the Church and then in the events in the world which challenge belief. He appears to begin and end by encouraging disciples to pursue the question Jesus put to his first followers 'Who do you say that I am?' Then he moved on to look at a path of personal holiness as exemplified in the teaching of the Sermon on the Mount (Matthew Ch. 5) given to us so movingly in the translation called *The Cost of Discipleship*, written in 1937. But by the time he came to write what is translated for us as *Letters and Papers from Prison* he had returned unashamedly to an exploration of who Jesus is for us in a world where the traditional and familiar practice of religion is no longer possible. In later chapters I will explore how Jesus is understood as displaying important characteristics of leadership. At this point in our journey it is essential to keep the understanding before us that Jesus Christ will be known again in new ways by each generation. Church structures and church leadership need always to be of the kind which will allow and encourage that exploration to take place.

## 3 A search for the tasks we are called to perform

Vocation or calling is not only personal. Many people offer themselves for work, including that of the ordained ministry, and are not accepted. In what can seem a rather harsh way a selection or interview panel say they do not recognize a sense of calling to a particular kind of work in that person. They say that they cannot discern God calling a person to this role and series of tasks. Much more positively, many others have work suggested to them. There is what is now regarded as an 'old' sense among many clergy that they should be 'asked' by their bishop to consider a move. To ask something for themselves shows an inappropriate sense of ambition and self-advancement. Nevertheless, growth and change can come about if they are open to opportunities when they present themselves. A 'timeliness' in any appointment makes the recipient and the people involved feel that the right person has gone to the right job. One training consultant I know uses a splendid phrase – 'the best person, in the best place at the best time'.

I understood the link between the person and the job when I listened to a lecture by the former Archbishop of Stockholm, J. K. Hammar on his fellow Swede, Dag Hammarskjöld. Writing about his appointment and subsequent work as Secretary General of the United Nations in his diary published as *Markings* there is this revealing section:

> In the inner landscape it is not one's own activity that impels one forward. Living a 'yes' in a 'now' is an acceptant stance that is prepared for the landscape to unfold and the possibilities that will then be expected. By Whom? Or by what? By someone – or something. *It is not we who seek the Way but the Way which seeks us. That is why you are faithful to it, even while you stand waiting, so long as you are **prepared**, and act the moment you are confronted by its demands.* (1955)
>
> *You are not the oil, you are not the air – merely the point of combustion, the flash point where light is born. You are merely the lens in the beam. You can only receive, give and possess the light as the lens does. If you seek yourself 'your rights' you prevent the oil and air from meeting in the flame, you rob the lens of its transparency.* (1957)

Some years earlier Winston Churchill had expressed similar sentiments:

To every man there comes a time in his life time, that special moment when he is figuratively tapped on the shoulder and offered the chance to do a very special thing, unique to him and fitted to his talents. What a tragedy if that moment finds him unprepared or unqualified for the work that could be his finest hour.

## 4 A strategic approach to leadership

Almost as fashionable as ideas about leadership is the demand for strategic leaders. We have always been familiar with the yearning for messiah figures as leaders who will defeat whatever is thought to be the enemy and who will bring stability and prosperity. What excites and energizes people is the sense that the organization they belong to is going somewhere. Strategic leaders can listen to those around them and then express their hopes in ways that connect. The leader with strategic skills can also chart a series of achievable steps to get to a desired goal. They can often pick a phrase or short statement which encapsulates what their organization is or what it wants to be. When I worked in the Diocese of Bradford the new bishop and his team, with the help of a media expert, came up with just such an expression of hope – *Future Faithful* – and even a badge to go with it.

John Adair has developed an important range of ideas about strategic leadership. He has written in a very concise and readable way in his book *Effective Strategic Leadership* just what this is all about: 'A strategic leader is essentially the leader of an organisation. An *effective* strategic leader is one who delivers the goods in terms of what an organisation naturally expects from its leadership in times of change.'[4] Later I will explore some of John Adair's other ideas but for now we need to record that strategic leadership is an important objective of our search.

### Be the church you want to see

From these four foundation stones or markers a confident series of next steps can be taken. They allow us to form a vision of a future church. Archbishop Sentamu spent a week in the summer of 2006 in York Minster fasting and praying for peace in the Middle East. In one of his talks in front of the small, lightweight, tent which was his temporary home he said, 'You must be the church you want to see'. Without a vision this book will be no more than an unfolding of good practice and lists of new ideas about leadership. With a vision, informed by research and energized by a right sense of restlessness, we can set out on a journey which will help us become the church we want to see. That church cannot be built unless there is a significant change in the ways in which leadership is understood and our ideas are formed. Appropriate adaptation can bring confidence in the processes of change and willingness to appoint broadly developed leaders willing and able to accept the challenge of re-presenting Jesus Christ for today and tomorrow.

## Notes

1. *Pulling Out of the Nosedive*, Christian Research, 2006.
2. Dietrich Bonhoeffer, *Ethics*, Fontana Library, Collins, 1966 edn, pp. 254–5.
3. Dietrich Bonhoeffer, *Christology*, Collins, 1966.
4. John Adair, *Effective Strategic Leadership*, Pan Books, 2003, p. 1.

# 2

# What Makes Good Leadership?

What makes good leadership as well as good leaders is the hot topic of the moment. When a group of people combine their gifts and skills as a leadership team a real buzz results. We all experience leadership and most of us are leaders in some part of our lives. What's new in our exploration is that we are looking at the many components which come together to make up what we call leadership. Part of our knowledge about leadership must come from our own experience of leading or of being led. There are some people who seem to have the type of personality which needs to lead from childhood onwards while others appear to be content to be led for most of their lives. Most come to leadership through the gradual development of their career. What is central to our current debate about leadership is that it is exploring new and different ways of finding solutions to the complex questions which modern life presents. It has moved on from the 'out there up-front' example of leadership solutions offered by particular individuals and has entered into a rich exploration of what can be achieved when people work together to combine their gifts and skills in groups or teams. Churches large and small cannot live and grow without shared understandings of who they are, where they are going and how they will need to be led.

## What is leadership?

Our modern word 'leadership' comes from an Old English word *laedan*, which has its origins in the idea of travelling together and making pathways through to a new place. It comes from ideas of people using their inner resources and joint efforts and collective wisdom to develop their lives. In modern terms leadership is concerned with ways of creating and achieving a desired future. Team leadership joins ancient and new definitions together because it talks about a people making a journey together. That means staying focused on the future as wisdom and tasks are shared in both good and bad times.

Peter Gilbert now guides business people through times of reflection in monasteries. He has been an army officer and a director of health care services. In defining leadership he says leaders must constantly demonstrate personal and professional integrity and an ability to be self-aware. He also says that 'a sure sign of someone who isn't a leader is when they look in the mirror to give praise and look out of the window and give the blame'.

John Sentamu, Archbishop of York, says that in his original language of Luganda leadership has a number of connected concepts. The word *omukulembeze* can mean the one who goes before; a pioneer; the one who clears the forest; the one who clears a path or who builds a bridge for others to cross the river. Here again we can see the range of interpretations of leadership. But it always means working with others to give a sense of direction and find a way forward.

## From individual to team leadership

The development of ideas about the formation and example of leaders is long and well documented. It begins in the popular culture and folk-lore of any country. Many of us will say that we know what a good leader is. The conquering hero is part of the history of imperial growth and expansion. A king or warrior rises from his or her people and takes them on to new heights of achievement and domination. Their stories tell us that this was done through the use of personality, taking over the levers of power and becoming the embodiment of an overall vision or direction which others would follow. Closer examination of the lives of some of these 'heroes and heroines' will show that they were talented strategists who knew how to put together a team that would build a vision with them. It is that experience we shall analyse and develop.

Our journey of exploration into leadership will be concerned with new developments in many spheres of learning. Churches can now benefit from much of this in developing their more comprehensive understandings of leadership. Moreover, Christian denominations and other faith communities have much to contribute about understandings of leadership from their values and traditions. Denominations and their congregations grow and maintain themselves, often against all odds and predictions, by using sophisticated survival and development techniques. We know how to adapt and change in gradual and resilient ways. We may be better at leading growth and development than we know. That is why there needs to be much more study of churches and their multi-faceted types of leadership.

## Many kinds of leadership

One of the most revealing experiences of my first months as Director of the Foundation for Church Leadership was to have explained to me the places where different kinds of leadership are exercised. This blew for me the idea that there is one way of describing what leadership is. Church members and church leaders, in common with many others, have a stereotype or caricature in their minds of what a leader is. Perhaps most likely is the military representative, heroic general and winner of battles, or the commercial merger king, or the person who has turned a good idea into a multi-million pound business, or the successful politician who has reinvigorated their party and turned defeat into electoral success. Or, of course, the charismatic minister with a popular church and large congregation!

Work with the Scottish Leadership Foundation, bringing in a completely different way of looking at leadership, has given me a broader understanding of the places where leadership is exercised and the types of people who can influence and bring about change. It is just one of many examples of how much our under-

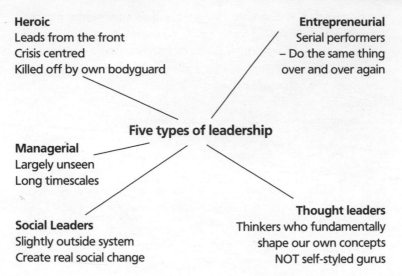

**Heroic**
Leads from the front
Crisis centred
Killed off by own bodyguard

**Entrepreneurial**
Serial performers
– Do the same thing
over and over again

**Five types of leadership**

**Managerial**
Largely unseen
Long timescales

**Social Leaders**
Slightly outside system
Create real social change

**Thought leaders**
Thinkers who fundamentally
shape our own concepts
NOT self-styled gurus

**Figure 2: Types of leadership**

standings of leadership can be enlarged by working together with colleagues and by forming new partnerships.

The tantalizing examples set out in Figure 2 concentrate on drawing different ways of describing leadership from people and examples in history and from our own experience. There are interesting ways of developing these ideas, with some real-life examples of those who exercise influence and are leaders in the way they bring about change.

**The heroic leader** is probably the best-known image of leadership and is seen in the self-confident person who has a clear vision of what needs to be done to get us all out of a perceived crisis and into a clear and confident future. We might think of a captain of industry or a political leader. Command and control is one phrase which has been used to describe such leaders. Recent leading politicians in the USA and Great Britain have made much of this style. They say, 'Let me describe the crisis to you and then show how I can save you from it'. Much more cynical analysts say that if there is not a crisis this leader will invent one.

In the end they will be deposed by rivals from within since they cannot continue to invent credible crises to resolve in a world which moves on and which they are less and less able to understand and analyse.

**The entrepreneurial leader** will see a good idea and develop it. They have an eye for opportunity and can build an organization around a new way or product. Such people also exist in the voluntary and public sectors. In the churches they are good congregation builders, good social project developers and good educators and trainers, as well as being good preachers and communicators. Such people have good leadership and managerial skills, but tend to repeat what they do over and over again. Once the vision and energy begin to wane, they may hark back to golden achievements in the past, showing that freshness has gone. 'When I was in . . . ' can become an over-used phrase.

**Managerial leaders** do not put themselves forward as heroes or saviours. They have long-term objectives and work away quietly and methodically at achieving them. Few such people will be remembered as models of anything but will have achieved more than many who made a lot of noise and created much steam. The post-war Prime Minister, Clement Attlee, was frequently described in this way.

**Thought leaders** are not the self-styled gurus who write the popular how-to books with easy steps to achievement and what appears to be clear analysis. Thought leaders rarely run organizations but develop theories and analysis which influence how we see the world, how we behave and how we understand ourselves. Albert Einstein had enormous influence through his scientific and mathematical thinking while Copernicus, Darwin and Freud were also highly influential thought leaders.

**Social leaders** are sometimes on the edges of mainstream activity or outside it altogether. They show us another way. This type of leader will not just see alternative, sometimes counter cultural, ways forward – they will create alternative organizations to demonstrate their ideas and vision of society. They will be driven by strong values and can communicate a picture of life as it could be. William Wilberforce and Martin Luther King are examples of such people.

## The search for leadership in our own traditions

What can these different kinds of leadership say to us as we search for new ways of understanding and developing leadership in our denominations? The churches to which most of us belong are part of historic and complex systems. They have their own ways of both resisting and of bringing about change. We begin with an enormous historical perspective and we have significant examples from our own leadership to draw on. We also know that our history and traditions can be as much a burden as an inspiration as we search for new ways of developing leadership in our churches.

At one level church life is experienced by most of the population of a country through its local congregations and clergy. What happens inside a church building is important for those who are attracted to attend in any regular way. What happens inside is also important for those who attend for baptisms, weddings and funerals since the building holds the memory of an important event in family life or personal friendship. The church building in a community represents history, memory, tradition and stability. Local leaders in the wider community will often work hard to keep a church building while not fully understanding its contemporary work or the pressures on the denomination which may not want to continue to use it.[1]

The story of how leadership has developed in the churches of Britain and many other parts of Europe is familiar to us through history lessons, art and architecture and our own continental travel. A thousand years ago many clergy were intimately attached to their local community with land to farm and tithes to collect, which gave them their 'living'. They depended on local generosity and the lord of the manor for their security. Other clergy belonged to religious orders and had a home in a monastery which was likely to be a part of a European religious network. The festivals of the church gave a structure to the year with its seasonal rhythm, while the calendar of saint's days gave the only holidays there were.[2]

In times of trouble or transition lay members of churches became aware that there was a larger structure. An archdeacon might make a visitation to see if all the necessary responsibilities of local clergy and congregations were being carried out properly. Very rarely a bishop would appear for some ecclesiastical purpose. It would have been clear to most parishioners that he belonged to a different order of society which took its leadership for granted from the lifestyle of the nobility. In earlier times saintly bishops had brought the faith and guarded its new converts and some had died for it. However, the domestication of this kind of episcopal leadership in medieval Europe came to mean that those appointed bishops occupied much of their time in courtly circles and not in their dioceses.

These local and national expressions of church followed the social stratification of medieval society. Those who became leaders had more than a general idea of who they were and what they were expected to do. They were born to it or were part of a social and political system where their friends, families and colleagues were leaders in other parts of national life. As the history of Europe developed so did the character of the local church. Secular influences were seen in the changes which took place in the church. Thus the rise of the prince with ideas of a local territorial domination meant that he wanted his local churches to reflect those aspirations. Eventually the 'nation state' threatened the very idea of Christendom and gave a much more local and personalized understanding of leadership to the churches in many parts of Europe. Those who rebelled and formed breakaway churches exercised leadership reflecting the core beliefs which had led them to separate from the mainstream of their society. Non-conformity had its own philosophical understandings of leadership, often in a highly personalized way.

In the nineteenth century, church leaders began to take a much more local interest in their congregations. Consequently their tasks and their desire for greater control of local leadership changed. The English Public School system which produced leaders for much of the British Empire also produced church leaders and missionary leaders with similar assumptions about who they were and how they should lead. Some were heroes, a few were saints, while to our modern minds many of them would seem intolerable and nearly impossible to live or work with.

Social or political perspectives on history are one way of looking at leadership. There are other ways which see such an interpretation of history and tradition as a barrier to the discovery of renewed leadership. Interpreters see that route as little more than an interesting background often containing descriptions of bad practice and inappropriate behaviour. We do know that present members of large organizations with long traditions can use their story to prevent change and use it as a justification for continuing what others would see as outmoded leadership methods.

## Character and values

Another way of looking at leadership is to examine the qualities which might be found in good leaders. From the inherited descriptions of leadership which I have given it is clear that the values and assumptions of a community will influence and inspire those who become leaders. This is as true in churches as in the rest of a culture. The development of character has become an interesting focus for explorations of leadership. This old-fashioned word may be a turn-off to some but it does embrace a range of concepts which have shaped civilizations and which are closely associated with individual, social and national values. When we say what we value in individual leaders we see how easily such words as 'truthfulness', 'loyalty', 'courage' and 'mercy' leap out. They convey concepts which we respect and expect to see in contemporary leaders. Such 'virtues' are seen also in their absence when individualism and power dominate and allow quite other sets of behaviour to be displayed. We condemn with a certain sense of self-righteousness untruthfulness, disloyalty, cowardice or recklessness and an absence of compassion or mercy.

There is said to be a number of personality or character flaws which are almost necessary for individuals who push themselves forward to become prominent public figures and sometimes leaders in their particular sphere. They are personality traits that are more concerned with recognition and power than with working collaboratively. Their dominance also strengthens an argument for teamwork and colleague criticism! Dr Thomas Stuttaford[3] has reflected on the characteristics of eccentrics who became leaders and says that at least four of the following characteristics are present in leaders who have achieved fame through a combination of personality characteristics or 'disorders': 1) they constantly seek approval and praise; 2) they dislike being anywhere where they are not the centre of attention; 3) they have shallow and vacillating emotions and beliefs; 4) they are self-centred, are short-term planners and become angry when frustrated; 5) they are inappropriately concerned with physical appearances and gestures; 6) they are overemotional when displaying grief or welcome; 7) they sometimes display sexual behaviour which is inappropriate; 8) they make speeches which sound impressive but which lack substance or detail.

We have already seen that the use of the word 'leader' also has an association with ideas and characteristics which are displayed by warriors – strength, courage, sacrifice, loyalty, truthfulness, obedience and self-control. Others come from the age of chivalry – mercy, courtesy and concern for the weak. When we add to these our modern essential values – respect for human rights and the autonomy of the individual – we have a considerable list of the qualities we expect when we examine the practice of leadership. It is even possible to say that these add up to the character we would like to see displayed corporately in a nation organized and regulated through its laws and governance.

I have sat in on some public discussions with military leaders about what is acceptable in the conduct of modern warfare. They say that they would not expect to lead their troops into conflicts using any other means than those which would be acceptable to the nation they represent or are defending. One of these leaders quoted to me a saying of Mahatma Gandhi: 'The means are the ends in the making.'

There are two other approaches to leadership we need to register and explore as we delve deeper into the discoveries and techniques which can support and inform new patterns of church leadership. They are the attractions and delusions of celebrity and of ambition.

## Leadership and celebrity

'Power corrupts and absolute power corrupts absolutely.' This well-known piece of received wisdom from Lord Acton has as much contemporary relevance as ever. We need to note here that too much exposure to unchallenged authority and power can have severely damaging consequences. There is a danger in leadership exercised by individuals or groups when there is little or no accountability or sanction. It is easy to be deluded by the trappings and the actual responsibilities of leadership in ways that are not at all healthy. Adulation and lack of critical appraisal can distort self-awareness among leaders. Too much media attention and manipulation by or of the media is a seductive temptation. Bishop Stephen Sykes has produced a thorough exploration of the necessary and appropriate uses of power as well as of the temptations and abuses that go with it. With great wisdom characteristic of his teaching and theological exploration he concludes: 'The abuse of power is better avoided by those who are completely aware of the temptations and have taken realistic steps to arm themselves against them'.[4]

The tendency of some leaders to put personality before ability rather than ability before personality has become a significant issue in nearly every walk of life. Modern media and instant communication have led to the development of the cult of celebrity and it is certainly true that many high profile leaders or would-be leaders rise or fall through their approach to the media. Many will remember the watershed event when John F. Kennedy and Richard Nixon appeared together in a televised debate. Regardless of what was said, the presentation of John Kennedy before the cameras convinced whole slices of the US population about who their next president should be.

There has even been a hint among the more 'frank' selectors of candidates for the ordained ministry that thoughts of 'how will they perform in public' have floated through the mind. The rise of synodical government as a major means of conducting ecclesiastical debate has produced allegations of a culture where 'those who perform well get noticed'. Studies of ministers set against the Myers-Briggs personality-type indicators have shown that extroverts are more likely to be chosen for high-profile jobs than the introverted but equally or more gifted candidate.[1] I examine this in more detail in Chapter 8.

Such cultural changes in how we perceive those who lead might raise an early warning about development programmes for leaders and about what is being looked for when senior leaders are being chosen. Whether it is prime minister or president or chairman or bishop or local minister there is a need to ensure that the development of a range of appropriate abilities, including those of team-work skills, are evaluated alongside any bias caused by the deliberate cultivation of celebrity. While an engaging personality and the ability to communicate are desired features of those who are selected to lead, they are not essential or core qualities.

## Leadership and ambition

Ambition can be individual or corporate and without it very little would be achieved. Yet in the churches, as with some other professions, there is ambivalence about appearing to be over ambitious. My own view is that wanting to achieve and to get a sense of satisfaction from a piece of work well done reflect an appropriate desire to be creative. This 'divine spark' we have within us is a gift and quality which comes to us as a part of our Creator's genius and design.

Ambition can be destructive when it takes over a life. It can be the death of good working relationships and, for some, of stable family life. In February 2006 *Time* magazine ran a feature called 'Ambition'. In it the lives of many currently well-known people were examined. For some it was clear that they had an enormous amount of energy and wanted to achieve from their earliest years.

Others showed no sign of a desire to achieve until some trigger came later in life which motivated their leadership abilities. Typically, the producers of the feature gave some contrasting quotes for the reader to balance their own views of ambition: 'Ambition is like love, impatient of delays and rivals' (the Buddha); 'Ambition, old as mankind, the immemorial weakness of the strong' (Vita Sackville-West); 'Ambition is so powerful a passion in the human breast that however high we reach, we are never satisfied' (Niccolo Machiavelli). Many of us will also want to remember and add a saying of Jesus about the first being last and the last first (Luke 13.30).

The follow-up letters in *Time* magazine a few weeks later were equally perceptive and contained many pieces of wisdom: 'Ambitious people don't just grab a bigger piece of the pie; they also make the pie bigger so that there is more to go round.' 'A focus on individual ambition is not healthy. If we ignore civility and empathy, we only exacerbate social decay.' 'Look at any troubled company or organization, and you'll find an excess of bumbling go-getters, who only make it harder for the selfless also-rans who really keep things going.' 'What about the pursuit of success in ways that do not result in money or fame?' These vibrant exchanges illustrate very well how appropriate and helpful it is to debate what we mean by leadership.

## Leadership in teams or groups

In this book one of my explorations is how and why leadership should be exercised in teams, with the leaders being important executive and representative team members. Across our churches the necessity to work in teams or groups has become increasingly important and at a pragmatic level some of the reasons for this are clear. The numerical decline of the clergy means that those who are stipendiary have to care for an increasing number of congregations. Some of these will span wide and different geographical or sociological areas. In urban situations the need to share clergy in the way that rural congregations have learned to do over several generations has come as a new and unfamiliar challenge.

For many clergy and congregations the preferred way to understand the role and work of a minister is a pastoral one. However, for effectiveness and the sheer imperative to survive, the need to establish new working relationships has become supremely important. Many clergy and congregations know 'in their heads' that working collaboratively as part of a team or group is right but 'in their hearts' they still want to operate according to a pastoral and more individualistic model.

Churches are not alone in experiencing the need to explore and value teamworking methods. When he was interviewed in a national newspaper on taking up his new post as chief executive of the newly merged Exel and DHL Logistics, John Allan said 'Successful businesses are about teams, and even the chief executive cannot be more important than the team.' When asked what leadership meant to him, his answer was 'Creating a team, setting performance standards and giving the business the will to win. When I joined Ocean [his previous company], my contribution was getting some good people together and giving the company a sense that it was going somewhere.'

If the experience of John Allan reflects the ethos of today's successful companies then we must ask what we can learn from this about leadership in our churches and what we can put alongside this strongly held view from our own history and traditions. Many of my colleagues across denominations in various parts of mainland Europe as well as in English dioceses and parish team ministries, groups, mission units, pastoral areas or clusters are raising one underlying question. They ask where the assumption comes from that working collaboratively is the right and best way to operate. It is my view that even a slight encounter with our biblical tradition together with examples of collaboration in establishing religious orders begins to hint at an answer.

## Leadership and faith

Can we really explore biblical models where at least co-leadership produced better results than command-and-control individualism? I think that we can. There are achievements of co-leadership where people have been more effective when working in partnership. Are the lives of Moses and Aaron, Ruth and Naomi, Elijah and Elisha or David and Jonathan ones we can use and learn from, even when things went wrong? I think that they are.

We can also draw from what was clearly an assumption of Jesus that he needed to put around him a group of men and women whom he came to regard as more than disciples. I explore this in more detail in Chapter 5. There are also examples of collaborative leadership in the most radical form of community life – the religious orders and lay communities – from which we can learn. Much of my consultancy work with religious communities would suggest this. I have been intrigued by the example of Francis and Clare in creating the Franciscan movement of Christian renewal. For the Vincentian movement the co-leadership of Vincent de Paul and Louise de Marillac is significant in developing a concern for the poor, as is that of Benedict and Scholastica in wanting to develop communities of prayer, work and learning. Many have looked long and hard at the experiment in collaborative living of Nicholas Ferrar and the community at Little Gidding. Add to this further examples from community work and from missionary endeavour and we will find stories of other kinds of leadership which could well provide theological foundations for collaborative working.

## Leadership and other faiths

The challenge, which in some ways is ever new, is for each of the major world faiths to hold to their core teachings and beliefs while continually applying those beliefs in new circumstances and situations. All faiths are now world faiths. Some are adapting from being dominant and over-arching in their countries of origin to being significant minority groups in other cultures. Others have aggressive elements within them which are hard to control. Whether in Northern Ireland or the Middle East the link between religion and local culture, rather than that of race, can have negative associations. Particular kinds of leadership are needed for these situations which have become increasingly stressed with acts of terrorism.

It is equally true for all faiths that the ethical dilemmas which modern life brings pose new challenges with consequences for the teaching and direction given by their leaders. There are ethical elements in modern life which are addressed by none of our scriptures while some received rules and commands do not fit easily with modern values and lifestyles. Only sensitive community leadership from whole communities of faith and from individuals within them can steer a delicate path through such controversies. Our own Christian leaders need to become welcome leaders and partners in this work.

## Can we trust our leaders?

Belonging to the postmodern influence which flows through much of Western society is the view that our politicians and leaders of large institutions cannot be trusted to deliver what they promise. Such an erosion of trust characterizes the context in which our church leaders operate. Denominational policies and programmes have promised much, not least in the area of church revival, but have delivered little. What needs to be done in order to restore confidence?

Air Marshall Sir Brian Burridge, addressing a conference of newly appointed strategic leaders in government service, IT, the public sector and the church reflected on the environment in which leadership is exercised today. He said that 'trust is a bank account' and if leaders are to empower those who work around them they have to begin with relationships based on trust. In an intriguing reflection on years of senior leadership he saw that the unravelling of complexity was one of the most significant challenges for today's leaders. There are particular qualities and skills needed by those who lead teams in our highly intricate and complex world. The experienced leader will generate trust in and beyond their team if they can develop the ability to analyse the factors and pressures which create complexity and offer some kind of analysis which is not over-simplistic but which will create order in otherwise chaotic situations. Basic to the development of order and the guidance of a team towards agreed goals is to want to invite co-operation from stakeholders. We cannot exist as local churches without working with partners and colleagues in our communities. We should not exist as denominations in a world of 'faith communities' if our will to work together is not greater than that which wants to keep us separate and divided.

Trust will develop around leadership teams if they can demonstrate an ability to take those who expect much of them through complex situations. It is not long since church leaders and evangelists were expected to combat 'the forces of secularization'. Now the complexities are quite different and are those of competing values and beliefs which can be picked up and pursued from any part of the world through our sophisticated communications systems. In a perhaps over-used phrase which adapts the fragile language of peace from the Middle East, the task of the local or national leadership team of a denomination is to develop the roadmap of faith which followers know about into a highway of possibilities for life which they can see and trust enough to want to follow.

## Good leadership conveys hope

One of the characteristics associated both with leaders and with leadership is inquisitiveness. In almost all the consultations I have shared with those in significant leadership positions there has been agreement that the best leaders and the invigorating leadership teams are the ones that are constantly asking questions and wanting to explore issues in new and imaginative ways. If there is one characteristic that would be agreed on in the development of leadership it would be this desire to be inquisitive and creative, to explore new ideas and to push boundaries forward.

In MODEM's book *Creative Church Leadership* many contributors explored what it meant to be a creative leader.[6] My opening chapter offered a theological framework based around the fundamental idea that, as well as leading us to understand suffering and death, God's purpose in sending Jesus was to enable us to experience resurrection life. I think this is a necessary characteristic of all those who aspire to share in the tasks of leadership. Creative leadership wants to take an existing piece of work or situation and transform it by injecting a range of new ideas and solutions. It is something of this newness that Harry Williams explored at the end of a book which influenced me much as a young priest, *True Resurrection.*[7] He distinguished between ways of longing for a different future in the use of the words 'desire' and 'hope'. Desire he saw as an extension of what we know already. Hope was for the unknown, the surprising and the unexpected outcomes. Good management can help us towards the achievement of our desires but good leadership can bring new and unexpected resurrection. Leadership within the churches needs to have these extraordinary qualities which can bring surprising new life to congregations, denominations and to any organization in which this quality is present. I call this creative resurrection leadership.

Leadership is not about crashing around in an insensitive way being creative and innovative without any regard for the consequences of ideas or actions. It is about timing, knowing just when it is right to make an intervention and a difference. This is the joy of the passage in the book of Ecclesiastes: 'There is a time for everything and a season for every activity under heaven' (3.1–8). Creative leadership does not give up when ideas are rejected or when told that this has been tried before in another form – 'It did not work then and it will not work now.' How many parish clergy and innovative congregation members have been told that? St Paul would have none of it and states that his reason for optimism and for hope was founded on his own experiences of life in a church full of the hope given by the risen Christ. 'Though our outer nature is wasting away our inner nature is renewed every day – because we look not to the things that are seen but to the things that are unseen' (2 Cor. 4.16–18).

The German-American theologian Paul Tillich discerned the difference for creative leadership in his book *The New Being.*[8] He explored biblical themes about the futility of all actions and the well-tried ways of the world which can break the most optimistic spirit. Describing what he calls 'God's timing' he wrote of the understanding experienced leaders have of knowing when to break a cycle of decline. He saw these moments as times when the creativity of resurrection breaks into our ordinary and often futile experiences of bringing about change. 'God's timing breaks into our human timing . . . the circle of vanity is broken' (p. 167). He saw the divine spark in such moments. 'The message of the eternal appearing in time and elevating it to eternity' (p. 169). Tillich is yet another example of a thought leader who brought new dimensions to our understandings of reality.

Good leadership has within it these qualities of inquisitiveness which lead on to the exploration of creative new opportunities for change and growth. These are frequently much more than an 'improvement' on what we already know. They are significantly different ways of understanding who we are and of how our companies, charities and churches might look. We are at just such a time now in the development of Christianity. It is clear that the old, Western model of static parishes with resident 'pastoral' clergy cannot continue without significant adaptation. We know that the desire for renewed spirituality is strong in many places and particularly among those who have great leadership responsibilities. Such people are looking for deeper wells from which to drink. We do not know what the churches of the future will look like. If we did they would not be churches of the resurrection bearing all the newness and surprise which such places will bring. We do know that such new creative places, where people will meet to be enriched and share visions of a renewed world, will not happen without the kind of leadership that works to develop these characteristics of resurrection hope.

## A new leadership highway

This search for new understandings of leadership shows that we are not alone in our churches on this journey. We are partners with those in the secular world of business and commerce who are experienced in studying leadership and also with those who want to include in their researches an academic study of church leadership. We have partners also among brothers and sisters in the other faith communities as they struggle to understand and communicate with the modern world. There are many pressing reasons why we each know that we need to develop new patterns of leadership. Changes and pressures mean that we cannot remain in our old ways, nor can we always take the pathways of gradual adaptation. Such a plea for partnership will, I hope, inform the many practicalities about leadership which I will be unfolding in other parts of this book. These opportunities to share are an exciting challenge which those in leadership will avoid at their peril. What's new in leadership is given to us by God. Our stewardship of this resource can create a learning path, and perhaps a highway, for those who know they must explore new ways of creative leadership in order to fulfil a part of the purpose of their life.

## Notes

1. *The Parish Church?* Ed. Giles Ecclestone for the Grubb Institute (Mowbray, 1988) has a very good exploration of the place of a parish church in its community.
2. This scene is described well by Eamon Duffy in *The Voices of Morebath*, Yale University Press, 2001.
3. 'Successful leadership is all in the mind', *The Times* 2, 11 September 2006.
4. Stephen Sykes, *Power and Christian Theology*, Continuum, 2006, p. xii.
5. See Leslie Francis and Mandy Robbins, *Personality and the Practice of Ministry*, Grove Booklets, Pastoral Series P97, 2004.
6. John Adair and John Nelson (eds), *Creative Church Leadership*, MODEM, Canterbury Press, 2004.
7. Harry Williams, *True Resurrection*, Mitchell Beasley, 1972, pp. 177–80.
8. Paul Tillich, *The New Being*, SCM Press, 1964.

# 3

# What's New in Team Leadership?

'Is this about real leadership or just the way they do it in the churches?' That was one reaction from a senior regional manager and churchgoer when he knew I was going to work for the Foundation for Church Leadership. A more general reaction has been: 'not before time', or 'Just what is needed in the churches', without being specific. Experienced leaders in commerce or the professions say more realistic things. After experiencing negative pronouncements about teamwork and strategic leadership from a church leader, one chief executive said, 'You will need to at least double your budget'.

There is no single answer to what makes a good leader. One answer for many situations is learning to work well with other people in a team or a group. My earliest experience of bringing a manager to meet a group of clergy is still the best – he said that 95% of what they did every day could be enhanced by support and training. There was perhaps the 5% which was spontaneous and inspired by the Holy Spirit which he could not help with! What we now need to explore is exactly what team leadership means. We need to look at how individuals are motivated by a passion for a cause or programme of change and how they can gain skills which will enable them to work together more effectively. We will continue to explore the dilemma about what makes good leaders, whether they are born or made, but in this chapter I will concentrate on what makes good leadership better through the development of effective teamwork.

## Why team leadership?

It is important to know what leadership looks like when people choose to work together in teams. There is a need to explore how teams work when there is little choice but to work together. It is becoming clear that working in groups and teams is a new and essential part of life in our churches. This is because of the pressures to keep traditional work going with fewer personnel and with higher expense. Teamwork is also essential because many special skills are needed to understand and lead congregations and larger units through the complexities of bringing about change. In church life the idea that ordination brought the ability to carry out almost any task has long gone. There is now a recognition that much more can be achieved when complementary skills are brought together to lead churches and to bring about change. The demand for more participation in decision making comes not only from the congregations and groups who provide much of the funding but also from those who enter ministry within the church, bringing with them already tested skills and experience of being leaders in large and complex organizations. In each of our denominations we are exploring how to devolve responsibility, and with this some elements of power and control.

The future for the development of many congregations is that they will be grouped together in some way, managed and supported by local ministry teams with stipendiary clergy developing new enabling, supportive and teaching roles. This situation demands an exploration of what is known already about the many aspects of forming and maintaining teams. Some of the contents for this chapter will not be new to everyone. I want to encourage you not to skip it because you have seen the ideas before. I have tried to incorporate some new reflections and commentaries on known pieces of work. What will, of course, be new in many church places is the practical application of these ideas. It is becoming essential to get into our bloodstream some basic understandings of what makes teams work and why they can be so much more effective in reshaping national and local churches for the work of living and sharing the gospel. We cannot quite yet say that 'the future is collaborative' but we are on the way!

## Shared experience of team leadership

What's new in church leadership is much the same as what's new in leadership in other walks of life. It is easy to see that the history and culture of our churches is both an asset and a drawback. It is an asset in that we have a perspective of change brought about through centuries of argument about principle and adaptation to cultural and economic forces. It is a drawback when a long history tends to conservatism and an over dependence on tradition and on solutions which have worked for previous generations. As with trends in other walks of life there are fashions in theories of leadership and their application which rise and fall. Some are pushed by 'gurus' who have charisma or who write in particularly appealing ways. A look at the books on leadership in popular booksellers or in airports or railway stations shows that the current most popular approach is 'six steps to success' or 'the ten steps you need to take to get to the top'. Then you will need 'five ways of relieving stress' and 'how to get more from life than work'. Such distilled wisdom does give pointers but those who have had to face the dilemmas of working with teams and turning round failing organizations say that there is no alternative to hands-on experience and taking time for reflection about what is going on.

Even though there is such an emphasis on team working this does not take away the human side of leadership, which often brings with it a sense of loneliness. Anyone who is given a level of responsibility will feel exposed. They will have their appointment resented by some colleagues and have projections or unrealistic expectations put on them by others. Does this sound familiar? The experience and the pressures are the same for those who are called to leadership in the churches. We need to bring our culture, heritage, traditions and values into the frame to help understand where we have come from and what still drives us on. Churches have experience and critiques to give as well as to receive. Some similar experiences and illustrative theories of how organizations work can come from the commercial sector and give real insights about how churches and congregations work. Other ideas, experience and wisdom come from parallels in voluntary work while others will come from colleagues in the caring professions and education.

I now want to share three significant ideas about team leadership. I will begin with one of the most important contributions yet made to the task of working effectively with other people.

## 1 TASK, TEAM AND INDIVIDUAL

Familiar to some will be the fundamental analysis of the components of team leadership developed by John Adair more than 30 years ago. Its genesis is interesting. Going to train future leaders in the army he found models and ideas about leadership which belonged to an earlier way of understanding people management, let alone warfare. Very rapidly he saw that what was important in leadership was how tasks were achieved through an interaction between both the work and the relationships of the people involved in carrying it out.

Like many brilliant ideas the concept is simple. There are three areas to which any leader has to attend. These are task, team and individual (Figure 3). What these words relate to will be

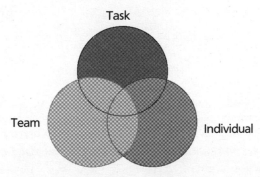

Figure 3: The three components of team leadership

described in the following section. To neglect or give too much attention to any one is to weaken the overall effectiveness of a leader and the development and maintenance of a leadership team. After two generations of application they will still be new to many who exercise leadership in our churches. They are directly linked to what we say and understand about leadership in our liturgies and in what we say a minister is called to do when they begin work with a congregation or larger church unit.

## Task

The purpose of any organization is to achieve a particular task. The clearer this task is the easier it is for those with responsibility to engage in the work and to be energized by it. When the task is not clear and those with responsibilities are neither motivated nor committed then energy tends to be focused on individual or team needs and the sense of purpose becomes obscured or even lost.

Task needs are

- to set clear targets
- to set standards of performance
- to make full use of resources
- to clarify responsibilities
- to ensure members' contributions are complementary
- to achieve the set targets or standards.

## Team

If those committed to the task do not have a high level of mutual trust then accomplishment will be difficult. Nevertheless energy can be over-focused on maintaining good team relationships at the expense of both the individual and the task.

Team needs are

- to know and respond to the leader's style and vision
- to feel a common sense of purpose with the members
- to have a supportive climate
- to grow and develop as a unit

- to have a sense of corporate achievement
- to have a common identity.

## Individual

The needs of each member of the team need to be attended to and respected. If individuals do not feel valued either for who they are or for what they contribute then the quality of the task and relationships within the team will suffer.

Individual needs: your own and those of others are

- to be accepted by the leader
- to be valued by the leader
- to be able to contribute to the task
- to know what is expected in relation to the task
- to be part of the team
- to know what is expected of you by the team

Why do I put this section into a book and chapter looking at what is new in leadership? Simply because it is easy to lose sight of a necessary balance when under pressure or when individuals are being particularly troublesome. Every leader will know the importance of developing clear and effective staff meetings. Good preparation, with task, team and individual in mind, gives an important template with which to prepare and evaluate such meetings.

I put it in also because the method of working, so well known to many who have received training, will be unknown to a significant number in the churches who have had no training in leadership. It is an ideal place to start, without jargon but with easily understood concepts and measures.

This simple Venn diagram also needs to be included in a section on what's new because those who become wearied by the weight of the tasks or the difficulty of maintaining the team need to revisit it over and over again. Failure to do so will result in a personal sense of failure or under-achievement or the impression that some individuals are being deliberately difficult. It needs to remain as a reminder to those who chase too readily after new ideas or who develop too much self-importance so that they may forget that they cannot achieve very much without the leadership authority given to them by those who work with, over, under or alongside them.

## 2 COLLABORATIVE WORKING

Now this really is a difficult concept for many in the churches. Do I really mean that? Unfortunately, yes, I do. Pages, chapters and books have been devoted to this method of working. I have spent more than half a lifetime delivering training and consultancy in order to develop understandings of it. On the face of it, Christian communities, congregations and organizations might be thought to have immense experience in working out how to communicate with one another and how to share tasks, including those of leadership. They might also be examples to the wider community of valuing gifts and skills from others. Yet 'collaborative' remains a difficult word. We need to look at why this is and at how a visit to fundamental ideas about vocation and ministry suggest how central is working in secure and creative ways with others to sharing and living the gospel message.

The development of collaborative ministry and collaborative leadership have long been a challenge to church leaders. Its qualities, requiring the ability to develop co-operation and the involvement of others, are looked for in the selection of ordination candidates and are frequently listed in the essential qualities expected of a senior leader. However, not all the models of leadership and the leadership styles of those appointed are particularly inspirational examples of collaborative work.[1]

Words used at the ordination of ministers and at the commissioning of church leaders have deep roots in our traditions. They come from the biblical sources which speak of leadership and from the history of our churches which discern that these are the pastoral and executive qualities of leadership required to sustain the life of a congregation and of a church. I will explore the leadership methods and attributes we see in the Old Testament and in the life of Jesus in Chapter 5.

## Task, Team and Individual and church ministries

'I am called to be a priest not a manager' writes Tim Harle in an International Colloquium on the work of John Adair. At this gathering at St George's House, Windsor, in September 2005 Tim presented a paper critiqueing John Adair's Task, Team and Individual. It is called *GIMME FIVE! Multi-disciplinary Perspectives on Leadership*.[2] Harle used an article by Jonathan Gosling and Henry Mintzberg in the November 2003 edition of the *Harvard Business Review* (pp. 54–63) as a starting point for his analysis. He also compared this with what was said in the words of the Anglican Ordinal, the service used when priests are ordained.

Gosling and Mintzberg offer five mind-sets to help managers interpret their world:

- Reflective: managing the self by reflecting on experience.
- Analytic: managing organizations by getting behind superficial analysis to essential meanings.
- Worldly: organizations exist in several contexts; managers should be found at the interfaces, or edges.
- Collaborative: not simply managing people, but the relationships between them.
- Action: managing change which needs continuity to give meaning.

Harle points out that the modern form of the Church of England Ordinal uses five models drawn from the Hebrew tradition which can be seen in the life and sayings of Jesus as recorded in the Gospels.

- Servants: recalling the words of Isaiah, as well as Jesus' self description as one who serves.
- Shepherds: Mediterranean shepherds lead their flock to pasture, caring for group and individual.
- Messengers: gospel, evangel, derives from the messenger who brought good news.
- Watchman: an alert, observing role.
- Stewards: caring for the rich variety of the earth's resources.

He sees a connection in comparing and developing the ideas and concepts contained in the two lists. Drawing from public sector comparisons he says that in the Church of today and tomorrow qualities which might once have been looked for only in the minister have now to be developed by the minister so that they become the overall characteristics of a congregation.

Task, Team and Individual might once have needed to be ingrained in the development thinking of a leader. They now need to be seen as characteristics flowing through the life of a congregation and especially its leadership team whether it is a church council or a smaller group who guide and direct the affairs of a congregation. For an effective ministry, those who have the roles of Servant, Shepherd, Messenger, Watchman and Steward now need to be Reflective, Analytical, Worldly and Collaborative.

## Building a collaborative team

Relationships are key to the achievement of any task and certainly to the growth of faith and life in a congregation. Tim Harle makes an interesting and important observation in looking at teamwork, collaborative methods and the place of the minister or leader of a group. He says that it is all too easy for the leader to give signs of working collaboratively when all the right words are used in putting together a team of people. The danger, reflecting on a possible distortion of Adair's emphasis on team leadership, could be that the leader creates a team of followers that he or she can dominate. Is the leader using their power to lead a team on to some vision of glory intended only to enhance their own reputation and achievements?

Nevertheless, Adair's Task, Team and Individual have stood the test of time and have won wide acclamation. They contain the essence of what group maintenance is all about. The common-sense wisdom which is contained in that simple combination of fundamentals ought to enable even the moderately competent to hold a team of people together without corrosive distrust.

Why is it then that the lessons are not learned from experiments and working methods which have been collaborative in the past? A number of recent pieces of research tell us that very many ministers continue to feel unaffirmed in their work and that consequently their congregations feel that they are not well led. Many senior clergy I visit tell me how powerless they feel to bring in the changes they would like to see.

## Strategic collaboration

A way forward comes from Adair in the development of his thinking and from those who have reflected on it. An important part of that development is that leadership has to be linked to strategy. This is close to what is called *purpose* by other writers and community leaders. Helpful ways forward also come from critical reflection on strategic leadership by Robin Greenwood and Hugh Burgess in their book about the way in which God's transforming power can reshape and renew challenging situations. They comment that *strategy* is not a word which produces excitement or even commitment in church circles. They say that it is important to ask why a strategy is being developed. The underlying motivations and hoped-for achievements have to be set out and given general acceptance by all those who might be grouped in the Task, Team and Individual bracket. Without meaning to do so, and while describing a different situation – that of impotence when leaders think they can exercise power – an interesting dilemma is revealed.

> Church leaders frequently disclaim their power to change aspects of the organisation; local people often choose not to see the wider picture; tensions and controls within the church are significantly more subtle than in any commercial organisation. Although the leaders of the Church may declare new policies, the cumulative effect may well be an empty church, rebellious clergy or threats to withhold income. In the light of our study on power, we can recognise that individual leaders are unable to effect results by exerting traditional hierarchical levers of power – statements, threats and ultimatums. This situation

therefore requires a much more subtle and holistic approach bringing alternative strategies into play.[3]

## Teamwork as a counter-cultural strategy

Working as a team may well be one significant way to counter a sense of powerlessness in the Church. This is because such a culture of individualism still pervades church life that teamwork can be suggested as something new, which still goes against much of the prevailing culture. Yet when skills delivered by different personalities work together to bring about change some of the subtle tensions and controls described by Greenwood and Burgess and many others can be overcome.

We now need to move on to look at the tasks and roles needed in the formation of teams and the delicate balance of personality which will make collaboration work. One of the most significant people to describe team and group roles or contributions and their fundamental importance is Dr Meredith Belbin. In Belbin's terms, different team roles are essential and can be delivered by different people working together in a deliberate and chosen way. Similarly senior executive staff cannot be effective unless they are put together as a group by an experienced and sensitive leader who understands the dynamics of change.

## 3 STAFF TEAMS AND ROLES

In church life tradition is strong and memory long. Those who want to resist change have, without being conscious of their achievement, developed sophisticated delaying tactics. It is only with the concerted approach of a number of team players that resistance can be overcome in a lasting way. A beginning in finding a way of moving forward in a 'stuck' situation was developed locally when I was an archdeacon. In two different parishes where clergy had been defeated or 'seen off' by entrenched local resistance I adopted a strategy which produced lasting change. Quite simply, just like policemen of old who walked difficult streets in pairs, I arranged for the parishes concerned to have two clergy. This is possible when a number of parishes are 'clustered' together and served by several clergy. The named vicar and the notional 'assistant' can both be present at significant church council meetings and on many occasions at major services and social events. A concerted effort by two such 'official' people with different temperaments and skills can hold resistance off and embody a new collaborative vision of local policy and achievement. They could then draw around them others who have the same concerns and begin to build team support. Such a strategy can work only if those in authority 'above' them hold to the same policy and do not allow the kind of representations to them that can undermine local agreed action. Such a piece of work does not necessarily have to be done by clergy but whoever is responsible has to have the active backing of senior people in their organization. Such a strategic placing of staff was recognized by Belbin in his series of observations.

Over a period of nine years Belbin and his team of researchers based at the Henley Management College studied the behaviour of managers from all over the world. Their different management styles were assessed through a battery of exercises and tests. Clusters of behaviour were identified as underlying successful work in teams. These effective cluster traits were given names. Eight and then nine team roles emerged (Table 1). The website www.belbin.com is a gateway into a whole industry of methodology and analysis about working in groups. The purchase of an entry into the wider website with these ideas allows companies, and could allow denominations, to access sophisticated team selection and development procedures.

There is no suggestion that team members are 'locked' into these particular roles. Indeed, it is observed that if two people have the same characteristics, then the less dominant one will adopt their second preferred role and use other strengths and skills. So that, for example, if a person cannot exercise their primary role of co-ordinator they might adopt that of resource investigator.

| Belbin team role type | Contributions | Allowable weaknesses |
|---|---|---|
| Plant | Creative, imaginative, unorthodox. Solves difficult problems. | Ignores incidentals. Too occupied to communicate effectively. |
| Co-ordinator | Mature, confident, a good chairperson. Clarifies goals, promotes decision making, delegates well. | Can often be seen as manipulative. Offload personal work. |
| Monitor evaluator | Sober, strategic and discerning. Judges accurately. | Lacks drive and the ability to inspire others. |
| Implementer | Disciplined, reliable, conservative and efficient. Turns ideas into practical actions. | Somewhat inflexible. Slow to respond to new possibilities. |
| Completer finisher | Painstaking, conscientious, anxious. Searches out errors and omissions. Delivers on time. | Inclined to worry unduly. Reluctant to delegate. |
| Resource investigator | Extrovert, enthusiastic, communicative. Explores opportunities. Develops contacts. | Over-optimistic. Loses interest once initial enthusiasm has passed. |
| Shaper | Challenging, dynamic, thrives on pressure. The drive and courage to overcome obstacles. | Prone to provocation. Offends people's feelings. |
| Teamworker | Co-operative, mild, perceptive and diplomatic. Listens, builds, averts friction. | Indecisive in crunch situations. |
| Specialist | Single-minded, self-starting, dedicated. Provides knowledge and skills in rare supply. | Contributes only on a narrow front. Dwells on technicalities |

**Table 1: Belbin cluster trait**

We all know how, in different places and situations, we behave in slightly different ways. Writing in a diocesan newsletter a local vicar gives a graphic description of how this can apply to a team of clergy and Readers:

> On Sunday mornings we need two people for each of our three main services. So there's lots of service leading and preaching! Each Reader has other responsibilities too. One works alongside the local hospital chaplain; another leads our Alpha outreach and is involved in prayer ministry. One has a pastoral role within the Old Town district. Another helps with the Sunday morning group for 11–14-year-olds. One is Deanery Financial Adviser and one Sub-Warden of Readers.
>
> We try to recognise and appreciate each other's contributions. Our meetings begin with a Bible study, the opportunity to say how we are and to pray for the church and one another. Of course there is the occasional disagreement but, genuinely, for the most part there is an exciting sense of partnership.

## More than tools of the trade

These descriptions of how to understand and analyse the ways in which people work together are not just simplified summaries from other people's wisdom. Nor are they secular levers to get the churches to change in a 'catch up or die', pressurized way. By quarrying our long experience of how people work together in groups and as congregations we can develop our understanding of the ways in which the Body of Christ works and how Jesus Christ can be known for us today.

The greatest contribution churches can make to what's new in leadership is to share some of what has made their durability their greatest strength. It may be that there are 'seven habits of effective churches' in the way that others have produced checklists for success, but we have not yet arrived at such a list. We may need others to tell us how good we are at survival and adaptation. Christians have learned how to reflect and to meditate; it is an integral part of our spirituality. In doing this we have a skill which enriches much more than our ability to deepen our personal devotion. The tools of critical reflection help us to 'learn how to learn'. We are part of an international movement and discipline whose characteristics help us understand how we can endure and develop through change.

## DECENTRALIZATION AND COLLABORATIVE LEARNING

Another element of what's new in church leadership is that we can now tap into a whole industry of learning how to learn. Reflective practice needs to be one of the core characteristics of any faith-based organization. One of the most influential modern writers reflecting on organizational leadership is Peter Senge. He has spent much of a working life from his base at the Massachusetts Institute of Technology studying how companies and organizations work. His 1990 book *The Fifth Discipline*[4] was called one of the most seminal books of the past 75 years by the *Harvard Business Review* and is regarded by enthusiasts as something of a bible. He defined the learning organization as '*a group of people who are continually enhancing their capabilities to create what they want to create*'.[5]

Senge describes himself as an 'idealist pragmatist'. He says that this has allowed him to advocate some 'utopian' and abstract ideas, especially about systems theory and bringing human values into the workplace. At the same time as he developed his research he tried to see how these almost intuitive ideas can be applied by people in very different kinds of organization. In ways which sound very like the task of many church leaders he says that his areas of special interest are in '*the decentralising role of leadership in organisations so as to enhance the capacity of all people to work productively towards common goals*'.[6]

## Learning as a team

According to Peter Senge, real change can take place through the learning experience of team membership.

> When you ask people what it is like being part of a great team, what is most striking is the meaningfulness of the experience. People talk about being part of something larger than themselves, of being connected, of being generative. It became quite clear that, for many, their experience as part of truly great teams stand out as singular periods of life lived to the fullest. Some spend the rest of their lives trying to recapture that spirit.[7]

Many of us can think of just that time and those experiences. Perhaps some of us are in that situation now. What is important in Senge's conclusions is that he could see that while everyone has the capacity to learn, the structures in which they function are not always conducive to engagement and reflection. His main teaching ideas spring from his conclusion that people lack the tools and guiding ideas to be able to make sense of the situations they face.

What distinguishes learning organizations from others is the display of certain basic 'dimensions' or 'component technologies'. Senge has identified five of these which, when they converge, give the work of those engaged in the team, group or organization that essential 'buzz'. The five are:

- Systems thinking
- Personal mastery
- Mental models
- Building shared vision
- Team learning

**Systems thinking** sounds the most technical and off-putting of Senge's characteristics. However, he says that it is the one discipline that integrates all the others. Its importance as both the fifth discipline and the integrating one led him to make it the title of his book. He says that one of the key problems with much that is written about management and leadership is that it applies rather simplistic frameworks to what are complex systems. Systems thinking looks far beyond those 'solutions' to immediate problems which, it is thought, will bring short-term results. Intriguingly, for us in the churches, Senge says that unless we draw 'systems maps' which show the key elements in an organization and how they connect, we will not be able to see the long-term issues and needs for change. One of the consequences will be cycles of 'blaming and self-defence'. Any help in getting the churches out of this cycle will enable many more ministers and leaders to survive and keep their sense of personal integrity and self-esteem.

To this basic need to understand systems thinking he adds the recognition that people are agents, able to act upon the structures and systems of which they are all a part. All the disciplines are, in this way, concerned with a shift of mind from seeing parts to seeing wholes, from seeing people as helpless reactors to seeing them as active participants in shaping their reality, from reacting to the present to creating the future.

**Personal mastery** provides the bridge between individual learning and the needs of the work situation. 'Organizations only learn through people who learn. Individual learning does not guarantee organizational learning. But without it no organisational learning occurs.'[8] Personal mastery is the discipline of continually clarifying and deepening our personal vision. It goes beyond *competence* and skills, although it involves them. Most interestingly for us, Senge adds that it goes beyond spiritual awakening, although it involves spiritual growth. Mastery is seen as a special kind of proficiency. It is not about dominance, but rather it is about *calling*. Vision, he says, is vocation rather than simply just a good idea about what to do next. This links directly with one of my foundations for leadership described in Chapter 1 where I describe my fundamental belief that vocational leadership and the calling to new work are linked.

**Mental models** are the 'deeply ingrained assumptions, generalisations, or even pictures and images that influence how we understand the world'. Such an understanding, requiring enormous objectivity, is just what churches in different parts of the world need as they try to reconcile differences over a range of social issues, not least that of sexual orientation. Again, Senge's descriptions come very close to a major contemporary need for the churches. He says we all need to 'unearth our internal pictures of the world . . . and hold them to scrutiny. It also includes the ability to carry on "learningful" conversations that balance inquiry and advocacy, where people expose their own thinking effectively and make that thinking open to others.'[9]

**Building shared vision** is the one thing, Senge concludes, that has inspired organizations for thousands of years. The capacity to hold and share a picture of the future we want to create is how people excel and learn. He says that what is lacking in many places is the discipline which will translate a personal vision into a shared vision – rather than the imposition of what a leader wants to do. It involves unearthing a series of shared 'pictures of the future' which will foster commitment and involvement.

**Team learning** sounds obvious but is far from it. It begins with the need for team members to be able to 'suspend assumptions' and enter into a genuine process of thinking together. He reminds us that the Greek *dia-logos* means the free-flowing of words and ideas through a group. When dialogue is joined with systems thinking, Senge suggests, there is the possibility of creating a language more suited for dealing with complexity, and of focusing on deep-seated structural issues.

## An important leadership benchmark

The real significance of ending this chapter with an unfolding of Peter Senge's ideas is that he turns around a basic concept of human experience. Through deep observation and studied collaboration a new vision has emerged. He saw that the traditional view of leadership was based on a false assumption: it was thought that people's powerlessness and their lack of personal vision could only be energized by the introduction of a new idea. Senge's great contribution to the fruits of collaborative working is to demonstrate that *in learning organizations the leaders are the designers, stewards and teachers.*

Creative, participative leaders are of many different types and are found in different places in an organization. They are responsible for building organizations where people continually expand their capabilities to understand complexity, clarify vision and improve mental models. That is the kind of leadership I wish we could all develop, model and share in our many and varied churches.

## Notes

1. I have explored themes of collaborative working extensively in my books *Understanding Congregations* (Cassell Mowbray, 1998) and *What They Don't Teach You at Theological College* (Canterbury Press, 2003).
2. Tim Harle, *GIMME FIVE! Multi-disciplinary Perspectives on Leadership*, available from 3 Manor Farm Close, Upper Seagry, Chippenham, Wilts SN15 5FB.
3. Robin Greenwood and Hugh Burgess, *Power, Changing Society and the Churches*, SPCK, 2005, p. 130.
4. Peter Senge, *The Fifth Discipline*, Random House Business Books, 1990.
5. Senge, *Fifth Discipline*, p. 5.
6. Senge, *Fifth Discipline*, p. 291.
7. Senge, *Fifth Discipline*, p. 13.
8. Senge, *Fifth Discipline*, p. 139.
9. Senge, *Fifth Discipline*, p. 99.

# 4

# What's New in Strategic Church Leadership?

It is always necessary to strike a balance between competing expectations of leadership in the churches. There is a prevalent view from committed laypeople with a concern for the internal and external workings of their churches that 'There is something wrong at the top'. Many who express this view cannot articulate just what it is they think is wrong. Some will give isolated examples of things they disagree with in church statements. Others will give examples of a church leader saying or doing something which has disturbed them. From outside as well as inside the churches there is an expressed concern that 'inexperienced and untrained people are taking big decisions'. If well thought-through reasons for dissatisfaction cannot be given but the feeling of unease remains then it is something else that is wrong with the leadership of the churches. It is that many clergy, congregations and members of the public who are interested, *feel* that they are not being well led. In an organization concerned with well-being, pastoral care and spiritual journeying this is a serious issue which needs to be explored. At the heart of the unease is a concern that there is a lack of direction in the leadership of the denominations. It is a matter of the right development of strategy.

The feeling that churches are not being well led can come from a variety of causes. One of the most serious is the gap between what congregations, local people and clergy imagine about the future of their churches and the views and pronouncements of some of their leaders. It is the responsibility of leadership to devise strategies and the processes and systems which will bring them into being. Their overall strategic planning must include the kind of policies, programmes and leadership that people will support and to which they can willingly respond. An editorial in *The Tablet* in the autumn of 2005 severely criticized a strategy for development and fundraising put forward by the Catholic Bishop's Conference of England and Wales. Good people, highly skilled and talented in other areas, did not have the background and the experience to produce a strategic plan which was credible and achievable. Among many strident comments, its editorial writer said that 'the people of God deserve something better'. There cannot be a stronger statement than this with which to express the *feeling* that there is something wrong in this particular area of leadership.

Not everyone in a denomination or in a local congregation can 'know where their church is going'. Most would not want to but do expect their local church to be well maintained and effectively run. The kind of conglomerate, cellular, organizations which are our denominations, contain such a range of different views that their leaders find it very hard to gain assent and agreement even for the most generalized of policies. People are members of churches for many different reasons and some find it temperamentally hard to agree with a consensus opinion. I know a bishop who says he feels that about half his diocese will do something because he asks and the other half will *not* do it because he has asked! I know a forthright superior of a religious order who said about trying to meet and reconcile the disparate expectations of the members of her community, 'I am damned if I do and I'm damned if I don't'. Nevertheless, that is what a leadership team is there for – to develop strategic planning of one kind or another.

## Strategic church leadership

Strategy is not a word much liked in church circles. There are good reasons for this. In the main, denominations are dispersed organizations which give enormous scope for local initiative. This means that a resistance to central direction, one of the assumptions around the word 'strategy', is almost integral to the organization. It is also likely that a church which holds together so many different viewpoints will be even more fragmented and in a more public way if opposing groups are coerced into taking a direction that is felt to belong to 'someone else'.

Professor Gillian Stamp describes the development of strategy as ways of bringing about 'the imagined or deemed future' for an organization or group.[1] She says it is first and foremost about values and dreams. This connects well with what a lively congregation should be praying about and debating. Professor John Adair says that what he wants to see when church people write about leadership is a view of 'the Kingdom of Heaven' in what they are saying.[2] This is both biblical in recalling us to the preaching and ministry of Jesus and a way of imagining the future in the present for which a resurrection faith yearns.

Even assuming that churches have a resistance to strategic leadership concepts it is important to explore what they mean and what they have to offer for a renewed church leadership. Adair, who has written more about strategic leadership than most, says that leadership is about concepts which arise from knowledge. A body of knowledge exists about leadership which has arisen from a series of questions being asked about why life is as it is and how progress and development are led forward.

Adair traces ideas of strategic leadership from their military origins in Ancient Greece. He tells us that 'strategy' is made up of two Greek words. The first is *stratos*, which means an army spread out or a large body of people. The second part *egy* comes from the Greek verb 'to lead'. Around 500 BC a senior commander in the Athenian army came to be called a *strategos*, leader of the army. The English equivalent is *general*.[3]

Approaching from a very different position as a leader in change management, Ketan J. Patel describes the tremendous pace of change which has shaped our modern world. In a very modern plea for strategic or 'joined up' leadership thinking, he sees the greatest changes grouped in a number of places, describing these as physical, emotional, competitive, monetary and spiritual compartments of local and international life. He says that the greatest danger is in the forces which are bringing about change being kept in separate and 'inappropriate' compartments. For him integrated or 'strategic' thinking is the only way for divisive forces to be contained and for creative activities to be fostered.[4]

Recent horrific terrorist atrocities have caused many to believe that reconciliation between world religions is vital to the development of just and peaceful societies. Others see the need for a spiritual revival in their organizations. Yet others want their leaders to understand and take seriously the place of religion in modern society. As I develop examples and illustrations later in this chapter I will take these needs as my main example when setting out my idea of strategic leadership and what it might look like within the churches. This is a deliberate choice. I could have taken examples from faith-sharing programmes or evangelistic movements or even from the programmes of renewal which newly appointed church leaders tend to produce. These pieces of strategy are described well and with greater understanding by many others who write about leadership and church growth. I hope that in taking a different approach and focusing on strategic leadership as it relates to the place of Christianity in community and public life I will be ploughing a distinctively different furrow. In some ways I have been prompted to do this following a significant and constructive outburst about the purpose of the Christian life by Professor John Hull. I know that this is dangerous territory which will further alienate some of my readers but I hope it will encourage others who are concerned about the overall direction that the churches in England have taken.

## What is the core business?

*'We looked for a mission shaped church but what we saw was a church shaped mission.'* This was the critical comment of Professor John Hull at the end of his 'theological response' to the Church of England report *Mission-Shaped Church*.[5] I will discuss its origins in Chapter 6 when I look at some contemporary expressions or local congregations or groups called 'new shape church' in their historical context. For the moment there is

another more significant question to be explored. It concerns the real and underlying agendas amid all the busyness and struggling for survival which absorb so much of the energy of those who are committed members of congregations. John Hull's critical comment well expresses the dilemma. My exploration will examine the different views of what a church or denomination exists for and will then look at how strategies of any kind can be developed. I begin by asking with John Hull, 'What is the core business?'

He shares his own feelings in a poignant postscript:

> I want the Church of England to become a prophetic church, a church which refuses to accept the poverty which is still so widespread in our society, that refuses to accept the marginalisation of so many disabled people, a church that accepts and promotes the equal ministry of men and women . . . a church that accepts diversity, sees the face of Christ in the other, a church that perceives the Spirit of God at work in the world outside the church, a church of the Magnificat (Luke 1.51f.) . . . Instead we have a church that sees little more than the creation of more and more churches, one that manifests an inability to perceive the church through the lens of Christian faith.[6]

There is no agreement about this and church leaders are beset by the tension between two polarized views of the work of the church. Is the purpose of the Church to lead its members towards a disinterested life of service in the world or is it a movement geared to win others over to its ways in a variety of faith-sharing initiatives? In practice, church life is concerned with both. Good leadership will embody tension and dialogue and articulate it by developing a vision which encompasses each in a way that is clear and neither confusing nor divisive. This is not an easy path to tread, especially when leaders have inevitably been formed in one tradition or another. When leadership does not succeed in holding different views in a creative tension, where no overall sense of direction exists, then all the feelings of unease come to the surface.

## A strategic checklist

There are concepts fundamental to the development of strategic leadership and these can come as new and fresh guideposts for leadership in the churches.

1 Strategic leadership provides direction – in faith and spirituality terms it has the fundamental purpose of reminding us of what journey we are on.
2 Strategic thinking followed by planning is the only way to ensure that things happen and remain in place to continue policies.
3 Strategic leadership relates the whole to the parts. In a church which all too easily fragments or which emphasizes only one part of its work, this is an essential element of its leadership.
4 That the sum is greater than the parts has to be true of the impact of an international Church with world-wide connections. Where leadership is 'joined up' with the thinking and action of church leaders in an international context an enormous amount of corporate energy can be released.
5 Strategic leadership can identify the qualities and abilities required for existing leaders. It can also point to the qualities and abilities that will be required in the next generation and nurture these.
6 Effective strategic leadership will get extraordinary achievements from 'ordinary' people.

While these may seem like six basic statements of effective leadership they are in fact more like the dissemination of a wisdom acquired by leaders in the practice of their work. No such body of wisdom arising from church leadership yet exists. We need to work together in much more effective ways to produce it. Not everything which is new in leadership is immediately applicable to life within our churches. What will be fruitful is a mutual exchange of experience in leadership from our different ecclesiastical cultures.

## Developing coherence

An experienced leader will know that there has to be a sufficient consensus around a policy if it has any chance of succeeding. To get there may need both charismatic leadership and repeated, systematic restatements of the need to move forward. What needs to be new and developed in church leadership is a concept of coherence where different ways of dealing with and processing change are brought together, utilized and understood. There are areas of feeling, intellect and intuition which need to be brought together for real energy to be generated (Figure 4).

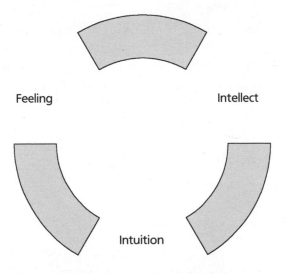

Feeling                                    Intellect

Intuition

**Figure 4: Integrated leadership**

## Pictures for the future

Ask most church members what they want their congregation to be like and they will paint some kind of a picture which may be about a 'golden past' that they want to see restored or an idealized view of an integrated and inclusive group. Ask clergy and some will certainly not give the same picture as a significant number of their congregation members. There are chasms between different perceptions of what churches might be like and it is no wonder that leadership which attempts to draw together and articulate a consensus, let alone a strategy, is hard.

Nevertheless, there are some stepping stones which can lead to leadership being valued by those with a range of different views. Task or mission-led groups can gain extra energy from sharing feelings about how resources are being used. There are some significant questions any church leadership group can ask:

1 Where in our activities is value being created?
2 Where is energy being wasted in unproductive activities?
3 Where is there latent energy which needs to be tapped?

A synod debate or a church council discussion around these questions will generate some heat. It might enhance the credibility of the leadership insofar as they are being flexible and allowing feelings and opinions to come out into the open. But the leadership will only retain credibility if it does something with the results of such a discussion.

## Developing a shared view of the future

One of the tasks, if not the principal task, of leadership is to work and consult in such ways that members of the congregation, circuit, deanery, diocese, district or province can feel that they have been listened to and that those who are their leaders both understand their concerns and express their hopes and desires. The model of leader as shepherd to be explored in Chapter 5 conveys a mental picture of the leader or leadership team who carry out this role. They have to guard and protect and to lead on to new pastures. But first the 'sheep' have to recognize the shepherd's voice and be trusting enough to get up and follow.

For many in the churches, 'hearing and responding to the voice' involves being given, or developing, a picture of what the Church, and local or regional churches, will be like in the future. Once they arrive at some kind of shared language and ideas about models of the future Church they can devise and debate plans – strategies – in order to get there. Part of John Hull's plea is that there should be a greater sense of trust and dialogue between those groups who should be working to produce a shared vision and then a strategy for building faithful communities committed to sharing in God's reconciling and redeeming work in the world.

## Strategic leadership and research

We know in practice that working together towards agreed goals achieves lasting change. We even know that the different skills which individuals bring to a group task will make it stronger and more effective than the sum of its individuals. Perhaps this kind of knowledge, which many call 'experience and intuition', is enough. Yet my experience says that this is not the case. We need to study why working together creates a better way. There is still a part of a nation's culture, and of the culture in our churches, which says that strong and dominant individuals will get top jobs. We next need to share in a rigorous exploration of how working collaboratively in a group or staff team can be sustained in its effectiveness. If this is not done there is always the possibility that, when under pressure, a leader reverts to another 'default mode' which is to lead from the front making individual and disconnected decisions without too much reference to anyone else. We need to be developing and then appointing leaders who are effective in using a range of styles and methods and who believe in consultation and the value of effective teamwork.

Such a search, which we can only undertake with colleagues, if we are to be true to our basic assumption, can lead to the development of a theology of partnership and collaborative action. It will have to be arrived at by an examination of our activities and of our tradition. Professor Jonathan Gosling and his staff at the School of Leadership in Exeter University have made a similar journey using different language. In the churches, we are beginning to talk of shared oversight in terms of shared *episcope*. At Exeter they describe this methodology as distributed or disbursed leadership. They have also looked at the place of the team leader and explored the concept of representative leadership within a team collaborative context.[7]

There are other important ways to describe this theological exploration. The Von Hügel Institute in Cambridge is using its Programme on Faith, Social Capital and Social Innovation, led by Francis Davis, to explore the practice of business ethics and leadership in a range of collaborative situations. The aim of this programme of activity is:

1 To identify and research striking forms of faith-inspired social leadership and innovation both by individuals and by organizations.
2 To see if different 'theologies' aid or hinder the practice of innovation or to what extent the innovation process is conditioned by social networks and/or social terrain.
3 To share striking examples of innovation, and the ideas and people that inspired them, internationally in order that (a) those seeking to engage with faith communities can understand their role, languages and potential and (b) that faith communities can scale the quality for their impact and advocacy.

The confirmed partners in this work are the Von Hügel Institute, University of Cambridge; The Young Foundation, London and the Hauser Centre for Non-Profit Studies at the Kennedy School of Government. In a creative way of describing this initiative they say that their aim is to make an international and virtual 'Social Silicon Valley' which is a theological workshop of social innovation in leadership.

## Spiritual and religious capital

I now want to share my strategic and different example. There are pieces of influential writing appearing from the denominations and from Christian research organizations which offer a new range of hopes for the contribution of churches to their wider societies. Some of them are beginning to use a new, and still to some, strange language or vocabulary. Their work points us towards the kinds of partnerships and relationships which will be needed for denominations to develop strategies for social engagement, the search for God's Kingdom, in the future. The William Temple Foundation has been developing work around the concepts of spiritual and religious capital. They say that this has been necessary for a number of reasons, each of which connects with the arguments for supporting a new kind of religious leadership in our churches.

The key strategic features emerging from their research programme – *Regenerating communities – a theological and strategic critique* – are these:

- There is a diverse spectrum of theologies leading to a wide range of ways in which faith communities engage with their wider societies.
- There is a significant difficulty in communicating with non-religious partners engaged in regeneration about the impact of faith-based engagement, and the theological identities and values which support and energize such work.
- The concepts of *spiritual capital* and *religious capital* have become ways of describing the reasons for faith-based engagement in social and political concerns to those outside the norms and concepts of faith communities.

They describe these terms with some clear definitions:

*Spiritual capital* energizes religious capital by providing a theological identity and worshipping tradition, but also a value system, moral vision and a basis of faith. Spiritual capital is often embedded locally within faith groups but is also expressed in the lives of individuals.

*Religious capital* is the practical contribution to local and national life made by faith groups.

In a stimulating booklet called *Faith in Action – The Dynamic Connection between Spiritual and Religious Capital*, Chris Baker and Hannah Skinner of the William Temple Foundation develop a series of strategies and policy recommendations which turn arid academic or theological terms into a strategic blueprint for action by faith communities in some of our cities.[8]

The strategic way in which the Church of England and the Methodist Church have taken up these ideas is in the theological and sociological underpinning of the development of their social outreach work. The report *Faithful Cities* is one of the most prophetic pieces of writing to come out of two historic denominations committed to being 'churches in the world'. In some ways it is a 20-years-on follow-up to *Faith in the City*, the report of the Archbishop of Canterbury's Commission on Urban Priority Areas published in 1985. It links faith and action in ways that immediately suggest the strategic partnerships appropriate for Christian churches who want to combine a search for the Kingdom of God with a life of faith in a Christian community.[9]

The Introduction to *Faithful Cities* by Archbishop Rowan Williams sets out the need for strategic thinking which embraces the development of leadership among the faith communities as well as within the Christian denominations:

> The resources of 'faith communities', now so significant in public thinking about regeneration and the fight against disadvantage, are not just a matter of assorted and ill-defined moral values; they are to do with what sort of a God is believed in and what awkward questions are made possible by such a God. It is a challenge we need to hear . . . and we should be grateful to the writers of this report for . . . setting it before us with such a wealth of narrative, analysis and vision; grateful also to all those who, by using 'faithful capital' in all the varied contexts of urban life today, have begun to show us what is possible for our society.

Strategic leadership is not just about reform and new directions within our churches. It is about forming faith-based, and sometimes faith-led, creative partnerships for the work of regeneration and renewal needed in our villages and towns as well as in our cities.

The Joseph Rowntree Foundation report *Faith as Social Capital: Connecting or Dividing?*, published early in 2006, and the Economic and Social Research Council report *Faith Based Voluntary Action*, have established faith as an important element in community regeneration. The leaders of these movements and the authors of these reports do not occupy easily recognizable places in the leadership of any denomination. Indeed, membership and representing any particular denomination may not be of great significance to such leaders. Nevertheless, impartial researchers and reviewers have acknowledged the value of this work in establishing the place of faith in modern British and European society. Further details of the research which led to these publications can be found on www.fborn.org.uk and at www.esrcsocietytoday.ac.uk. They argue for the development and appointment of leaders who come from or understand the faith tradition and who can equip and lead their people to make confident contributions in places where the value of spiritual and religious capital is welcomed.

## Practical examples of change leadership

The William Temple Foundation report has, among many other mind-stretching ideas, proposed three types of social capital which strategically led local faith groups can contribute:

- *Bonding* refers to those relationships that reinforce similar identities based for example on family, ethnic identity, class or gender.
- *Bridging* describes more outward looking relationships that create bridges with other groups of different cultural, social, economic and political status.
- *Linking* measures the ability of an individual or community's networks to 'link up' to other networks to access power and resources that they could not acquire on their own.

The first recommendation of *Faithful Cities* is that the Church of England, with its ecumenical partners, must maintain a planned, continued and substantial presence across our urban areas. I could refer to other reports about market towns and the countryside which argue for the same thing – planned, co-ordinated, strategic action and use of resources. Strategic thinking is about recognizing and encouraging signs of God's Kingdom in the world. It requires as much energy, research and time as any other work that might be called strategic within our churches.

## Levels of change

Ideas sink in to us gradually. We all know the shock of having to get used to a new situation in our personal life. Just the same is true when the communities and networks we belong to have to change. Elements of resistance and denial of the need to change lurk under the surface and sometimes bubble up in angry outbursts. There is a healthy cynicism in church circles about change. Long-term members of a congregation, diocese or denomination will have experienced new ideas which rise and fall as new leaders arrive with their new ideas and solutions. Inertia and outright resistance can sap energy when leaders try to bring in adaptations and solutions designed to move a people on from what they may see as stagnation or decline. In a very direct talk about leadership in a political and cultural context the former minister for Media, Culture and Sport and Director of the Clore Foundation, Chris Smith, made this list:

1 Know what the central direction is going to be and develop stories to illustrate how to get there.
2 Keep an awareness of what the 'big picture' is and persist with particular issues in order to overcome obstacles.
3 You cannot succeed unless you are prepared to fail in some areas.
4 Great leaders show their vulnerability from time to time.
5 Know yourself – your strengths and weaknesses and what drives you.
6 Leadership is about building relationships.
7 Never run out of enthusiasm.

Three words seem to emerge from that list as core strategic elements in the work of a leader or of a leadership team – *direction, relationships, enthusiasm.* How these are translated into policies rammes which a majority will affirm and support is the at needs to be new in church leadership. Many will say it is the key to knowing about any form of strategic leadership. When achieved it is the 'silver bullet' which gives the feeling that an organization is going somewhere because it is being well led. There is a diminution in the experience that those who are the leadership are in some way inadequate for the task. The bridge to this achievement is the ability to devise an agreed strategy and to drive it in a way that others will follow and in the process feel affirmed and developed.

## Giving a sense of direction

The greatest contributory factor to feelings of ineffective leadership is the sense that the organization is not going anywhere. Even if the purpose of a church is to 'manage decline', there must be a sense of direction and a plan. For leadership within the churches one of the new factors is how to be realistic about the direction of faith in its institutional form. John Hull's criticism was real and well expressed as a challenge. Can churches renew themselves internally while expending much or most of their energy in service to the world? It can seem like a juggling act with dangers and pitfalls all around.

## Building relationships

Stafford Beer and John Beckford have developed an appropriate diagram from concepts of life in participative organizations which describes the balance of tasks and the place of responsible leadership (Figure 5). This has enormous resonances and well expresses what new church leadership needs to understand.

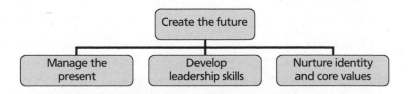

Figure 5: Balanced leadership

My own testimony to the effectiveness of these concepts comes from my time as an industrial chaplain in the 1970s and 1980s. I began my work in South Yorkshire, Sheffield and Rotherham, with many of the companies I visited being part of the British Steel Corporation. A large slice of the works in this group had formerly been owned before nationalization by United Steels. Stafford Beer had been Production Controller and the founder of the Operations Research Group, first at the Samuel Fox works in Stocksbridge and then in a new organization called Sigma (Science in General Management Ltd) based in Sheffield. His influence, with that of many others, encouraged by the culture of that company, was still prevalent in my days there.

The process of managing the present while creating the future is enormously challenging work for any leader or leadership team. Such terms and tasks will be familiar to any minister, bishop, chairman or moderator in a range of denominations. The key, alongside the continuous development of leadership skills, is the method of nurturing the 'core values' of the organization. These will include the original foundation values of the organization – what has come from the Wesleys or from Martin Luther or what comes from the centuries-long tradition of teaching by papal Encyclical. Alongside these comes the question from Dietrich Bonhoeffer which I have asked again and explored elsewhere, 'Who is Jesus Christ for us today?'

A lively interchange of the Stafford Beer concepts allows for those who are in the leadership team to maintain a sense of clarity. Each task is a different one and needs attention by all of the team at some time. On other occasions some members will take particular responsibilities while the representative figure who is the team leader will express the vision of them all.

## Creating enthusiasm

My own diagram comes as a conclusion to these thoughts about what needs to be new in developing strategic church leadership. It is the plea for continuing reflection on what is happening to the congregation, diocese, region or denomination. Objectivity is the key. Team leadership, with the use of experienced consultants, enables a monitoring of the examples and ideas I have described above. Values, direction and process are vitally important. They are expressed in this way:

- What do we believe in?

  - Where are we going?

    - How do we get there?

Strategic leadership contains that essential spark of genius which can interpret complexity in a way that will allow team members and followers to see that order has been brought out of complexity. Collaborative leadership is much more easily talked and written about than done. Developing deeper understandings of it is part of the new work of a learning church. There is no doubt that in many of our leading companies and organizations teamwork and collaborative work in groups is seen as fundamental to success. In our churches we begin with our own culture and traditions. We also begin with our own understandings of hierarchy and of leadership. We now have to take our own confident steps along this new path to collaborative strategic leadership.

Our beliefs will tell us much about the core values which need to be unearthed so that new understandings of leadership can be reinforced. We have rich biblical traditions which inform us, including leadership stories of a people being led through wilderness times. We have intriguing accounts of the development of leadership from Judges to Kings. Alongside this tradition we have the fiery accounts of the lives and disturbing messages of the prophets, many of whom were more comfortable 'leading from the edge'. We have our New Testament tradition of Jesus being recognized by, and perhaps growing out of, the prophetic tradition of John the Baptist. We have the key developmental texts of the ways in which Jesus selected and worked with his disciples. In the Acts of the Apostles and the Epistles we have stimulating accounts of how a young organization, the church, grew and developed. How leadership was exercised so that growth continued through a series of internal disputes is the story of the Early Church. That biblical narrative of what we believe in, where we are going and how we get there, is what we shall explore next as we look at leadership in the Bible.

## Notes

1. Gillian Stamp, Director of the Brunel Institute of Organizational and Social Studies (BIOSS), The University of West London. Reflection made during a consultation at St George's House Windsor.
2. John Adair, *Creative Church Leadership*, Canterbury Press Norwich, 2004, p. 8.
3. John Adair, *Effective Strategic Leadership*, Pan Books, 2003.
4. Ketan J. Patel, *The Master Strategist: Power, Purpose and Principle*, Hutchinson, 2005.
5. John Hull, *Mission-Shaped Church: A Theological Critique*, SCM-Canterbury Press, 2006.
6. Hull, *Mission-Shaped Church*, p. 36.
7. This is described in an engaging booklet, *What is Leadership? Theories of Leadership*, p. 12, which can be downloaded from the Exeter School of Leadership website, www.leadershipsouthwest.com.
8. Chris Baker and Hannah Skinner, *Faith in Action – The Dynamic between Spiritual Capital and Religious Capital*, William Temple Foundation, 2006.
9. *Faithful Cities: A Call for Celebration, Vision and Justice*, Church House Publishing and Methodist Publishing House, 2006.

# 5

# What's New in Leadership from the Bible?

The Bible is a gallery of portraits about leadership. Its different books contain accounts of practically every type of leadership style imaginable. In addition to personalities and their exploits and adventures there are significant pieces of reflection on the place of leadership in the life of new and developing communities and nations. These portraits come to a climax in God's purposes in sending Jesus Christ. He embodies personality and purpose in leadership. He selected a diverse team of people and through patient encouragement enabled them to achieve much more than might have been expected. He transforms some strongly held ideas and caricatures of leadership. From the time of the resurrection those who were establishing new Christian communities had to work in the light of these sometimes radical reinterpretations.

There is a kind of leadership which has an authority all of its own. When the Roman Centurion met Jesus he recognized him as a leader who worked under authority just as he did. In the story recorded by St Luke (7.2–10) and St Matthew (8.5–13) the centurion makes a series of comparisons with his task and mission and that of Jesus. They were both people under authority. The centurion had been charged with tasks by his superiors and by the Roman state. The conversation the two men had was about how they were discharging their responsibilities. The centurion had the weight of command. When he gave orders his men obeyed but he himself was under orders and had to discipline himself so that he could carry out his tasks. He saw that

75

s was acting under God's authority, was motivated and focused, and was well aware of the weight of that responsibility. Jesus also had to follow God's 'orders' and point his followers in the directions that authority required.

Just one short biblical reflection demonstrates in a very direct way that leaders and leadership are present in roles and themes throughout the scriptures. What is new for us is to look at familiar stories and passages in ways which will allow leadership themes to leap from the pages. Some titles and ideas about leadership will be familiar but Bible commentaries normally have little to say about leadership and some books about Jesus do not even have it in their index! Other passages will need to be teased out in order for us to be able to see their enormous significance for individual leadership responsibilities and for the energizing characteristics of leadership which we are discovering for teams and groups. The tour of our portrait gallery will only allow space to look at the most notable examples of different kinds of leadership – the Gandhis and Mandelas of the Bible.

## Well-known leadership titles

A range of portraits and demonstrations of leadership exist in the Old Testament. Some of these images and examples were picked up by Jesus as ways in which he would shape his own ministry. They remain as models developed by emerging leaders in the Early Church as they tried to create structures and ways of operating after his example. Some traditional understandings of leadership were given profound new meanings and interpretations by Jesus. We are familiar with many of the titles he used and remodelled. A brief exploration of their use will enrich our contemporary attempts to create ways in which Christian leadership can be exercised.

## Steward

Our portraits of leadership from the scriptures begin with the word 'steward'. Ideas of stewardship of the created order emerge in the responsibilities given to Adam and Eve after their expulsion from the Garden of Eden. The story in the first chapters of the book of Genesis is a familiar one. Almost all those who describe key characteristics of leadership begin by saying that inquisitiveness is present in the restless search for change and improvement, or even for solutions. Adam and Eve had that characteristic. Eve wanted to explore why eating the apple which would give the knowledge of good and evil was forbidden. The consequence of her inquisitive search was that humankind was given responsibility for the oversight of the created order. Inquisitiveness and responsibility go together in this story and make a fundamental characteristic of leadership. Work becomes both a joy and a curse, but stewardship of the creation they had helped to name was inescapable. Eating the forbidden fruit gave both responsibility and authority.

At the very beginning of our exploration of the authority which God gives to a people we come across this key concept of steward. The late Lawrence Nevard, founder of the once flourishing Leadership Development Group, thought that stewardship was closer to our understandings of management than of leadership. He says a steward is someone who manages, administers or supervises.[1] The word 'steward' occurs a number of times in the Old and New Testaments. When Joseph, in exile in Egypt, greets his brothers he instructs his steward to prepare a meal (Genesis 43.16ff.—44.13). This was clearly the person responsible for organizing the affairs of the household. In the New Testament the content of a steward's job is made clearer. Chuza was a steward in Herod's household (Luke 8.3). The steward was responsible for paying the labourers who worked in the vineyard (Matthew 20.8, 9). Jesus told the story of the dishonest steward who was squandering his master's assets (Luke 16.12). Jesus asks Peter, 'who is the trusty and sensible man whom his master will appoint as his steward, to manage his servants and issue their rations at the proper time?' (Luke 12.42). The steward as manager is the leader who shapes structures in order to make sure that a vision delivers its promise.

Those who can accept authority and organize an efficient

organization are people who 'the master' can trust with weighty and more serious things. I like Nevard's description of the steward-manager, for us the team leader and organizer, 'Getting things done through other people'. Joseph's steward did all this. He was the manager of Joseph's household. He was also trusted to hold the conversation with Joseph's brothers when they discovered that treasures were in their travelling sacks and that they were in danger of being accused of theft. He conducts a conversation with skill and tact thus enabling the next stages of the saga to unfold. Many of those in responsible positions have first proved themselves by being good managers and have worked in close co-operation with their senior leaders enabling plans to be put into effect. Good leadership is also about good management.

## Judge

This is the earliest form of leadership by oversight we find in the Bible. Here communities give their support to people who display wisdom in dealing with public affairs. Judgement is an essential part of the quality and responsibility of any leader or leadership team.

Judgement runs alongside law in the Old and New Testaments. The word originates from the situations in which people went to their local shrine when they needed a ruling from God on any matter either of faith or practice. The cult official would give 'judgement'. If the question was a new one then a sacrifice would be made or a sacred lot cast if the official were a priest. If they were a prophet it would be by a dream, a vision or in ecstasy. The resulting judgement was called a *torah* and would be used as a precedent if the question came up again.

Judges at this time represented a wide interpretation of leadership. As well as their tasks of legal arbitration and administration judges were often military leaders, some of whom became judges having won their reputation as wise people on the field of battle. Gideon was one such judge. He had a charismatic quality as well as a reputation for wisdom. In the book of Judges Chapter 12 we read that 'the spirit of the Lord came upon Gideon' showing that he carried a kind of authority which was recognized to be more than that bestowed by human respect and acclaim. At this stage in the history of Israel that kind of divine blessing or charisma seemed to 'last as long as it lasted'. Once talent and support waned the people looked for someone else to take on the mantle – a kind of support not unlike the fate of many in public, political and commercial life today.

Following the leadership of Moses and Joshua the Israelite tribal confederacy was organized and led for approximately 44 years by a succession of 12 Judges. These leaders came to public notice at times of crisis when their ability to lead was recognized and accepted by their people. Judges came from individual tribes but their authority was so respected by the whole confederacy that they can rightly be called leaders in a collective way at this stage in the development of Israel.

Judges were significant people in Israel and had power and influence before there were kings. Samuel was a judge over Israel. When he grew old he appointed his sons as judges but they were not worthy of the name (1 Samuel 8.1). As a result the elders came to Samuel and asked for a king. The delightful conversation in Chapter 8 tells of how God asked Samuel to set out for the people what it would be like under a king. There was a danger that they would lose much of their freedom and many of their possessions as kings grew in stature and wanted to enhance their worldly status. Unfortunately the people did not want to learn the lessons of the corrupting nature of absolute power. Consequently Samuel anointed Saul as the first King of Israel. His predictions were accurate and later God had to have a second talk with Samuel which resulted in his anointing David. It was not until the time of David's successor, Solomon, that wisdom and kingship were united in an almost legendary way.

## Anointed

'. . . and some have greatness thrust upon them.'

That leadership of any kind had a link with the authority bestowed by God was displayed at an early stage in the Bible by a ritual of anointing. This gave another dimension to the place of a leader in society. Even now, the whole selection process for candidates in the ordained ministry is based on the idea that the church calls men and women to particular roles and tasks. It is recorded that, when they had been anointed, both Saul and David were seen to 'have the spirit come upon them mightily' (1 Samuel 10.6ff.—16.13).

The word for anointing in Greek comes from the word 'chrism', and was a mixture of olive oil and the scented balsam. Old Testament kings and priests were anointed when they began their work to symbolize that they were endowed with particular spiritual gifts and that they had God's blessing for their work. The hope for a deliverer for Israel in the later parts of the Old Testament was described in the hope of the coming of the anointed one or in Hebrew, Messiah. Jesus was called Christ because he was seen as this 'anointed one'. His followers came to be called Christians because they were followers of this Christ, the anointed one.

Throughout John's Gospel Jesus is referred to as the Christ, the anointed one, though there are fewer such references in the other Gospels. At his trial much hinges on the question put to Jesus, 'Are you the Messiah?' In Mark 16.41 he admits that he is. However, in Matthew and Luke he refuses to answer. There is some devout speculation that when Mary anoints Jesus' feet with precious oils she anoints him and is preparing him for a kingly death (John 12.1–3). Whether or not this is the case at this point in his ministry she certainly recognized both his authority and his divine leadership.

In Britain monarchs are anointed as part of the coronation ritual. There is now a long tradition of the monarch, as the anointed one, showing humility and coming to a cathedral, the seat of the bishop, symbolically to wash the feet of the poor on Maundy Thursday. The day gets its name from the Latin words *mandatum novum* (John 13.34), the 'new commandment' which Jesus gave to his disciples 'that you love one another as I have loved you'. The deliberate actions of an anointed king give the whole event the appropriate aura of servant leadership. It is the act of humility which rings truest in the Maundy and anointing ceremonies. They strike a contrast with the trappings and dangers which come with power and grand titles.

Anointing with oils has now come back into prominence and used in many denominations. It gives a powerful, and sometimes, aromatic, symbol at an important time of transition in the life of an individual and conveys a sense of recognition by the whole community. Anointing is now an essential part of ordination services for Anglican as well as Roman Catholic clergy. In this way they receive a symbolic sign that they are both blessed by God and set aside for a special role in society. Oils of anointing are also used at baptisms and in services of confirmation.

## King

The concept of kingship with different public roles and responsibilities has been adopted at a particular time in a people's history when they needed representative figures as well as leaders who could give wisdom and carry out executive duties. Modern monarchs live leadership in different ways. Like some of the roles of executive leaders, they carry out representative functions. It is often by their actions and gestures, performed as they live out their role, that monarchical rulers carry out symbolic as well as actual tasks. Some similar functions are attached to the public roles of bishops and clergy.

David was the second king to rule over Israel once the monarchy had been established. Gideon had turned down the request from the confederation of tribes that he should become their king. His reasoning was that Israel had already a king in Yahweh and it was therefore unlike other nations. Samuel's response had been the same, arguing that such a move would 'secularize' Israel and therefore lessen the status of Yahweh. There was, however, a developing argument that by making Israel a kingdom it could be properly called a nation, which would allow God to speak to other nations through it. Samuel gradually became persuaded by the argument and anointed Saul as king, thus recognizing the need for a representative figure as the embodiment of a new nation state.

When David succeeded Saul his leadership helped to consolidate the identity of a new nation. Having shown himself to be a successful military leader in the southern confederation of tribes he sought to extend his authority to the northern tribes as well. As an emerging national leader he had to renegotiate, and limit, the independence of the individual tribes in order to create a central focus for religious and political leadership. He was also a charismatic leader who knew the importance of symbolic gestures. Consequently, he brought the Ark of the Covenant, the symbol of the presence of God, to the new capital of Jerusalem.

Having centralized power in both spheres he then took steps to bring all of Israel's life under his control. Against the advice of his counsellors he followed his leadership intuition and had a census taken of all Israel. Like William the Conqueror and the census which became the Domesday Book he needed to know what he had before he could decide how best to administer it. Consequently it is thought that King David was behind the division of Israel into administrative districts which did not always coincide with tribal boundaries. In this way he established his own power base and was able to appoint his own devolved leadership team. He was then able to use his patronage to distribute the responsibilities for administering his territories.

Jesus was also described as a king. The Gospel writer Matthew, addressing his text to the Jewish people, saw it was important to emphasize that Jesus as king was connected through direct family lineage to King David. He gives a genealogy to prove it (Matthew 1.1–17). 'King of the Jews' was one of the titles which perplexed Pontius Pilate when Jesus was brought for trial (Matthew 27.27–31) and one which annoyed the chief priests and rulers of the synagogue. After his trial soldiers mocked Jesus, putting on him the scarlet robe and crown of thorns shouting 'Hail, King of the Jews!' This title of king formed part of the inscription on the cross when Jesus was crucified (Matthew 27.37). From the strength of the narrative it does seem that this title was one which had been used, if only in the streets and among the crowds, about Jesus.

What is most interesting, especially in the accounts of Jesus' last days, is that he interpreted the power and authority which would come with kingship in quite different ways. The images of servant and of shepherd were those which seemed to give strength to his actions. Many of us will be familiar with a modern hymn with words which tell this story for today with the title 'The servant king'. When reading through the materials given to me for safe keeping by the Leadership Development Group I came across a title for one of their essay competitions which sums up in a very visual way how authority and acclamation can be received without distortion of personality or of purpose: 'A Christian has a king who rides on a donkey.'

## Shepherd

The world of the Bible is predominantly a rural one so it comes as no surprise that sheep with their shepherds supply strong examples and imagery throughout. There are almost 700 occasions when the words 'shepherd', 'flock' and 'sheep' are used in the books of the Bible. Only 100 of these are in the New Testament. King David began as a shepherd and endowed this image of leadership with special significance.

The background for much of the imagery around shepherds as leaders comes from the context in which they worked. Sheep wandered because they were not kept in fields but searched for food often in very sparse countryside. Shepherds were necessary to guide their flocks on to richer pastures. The scattered nature of the flocks meant that they were prey to wild animals and the shepherd had to anticipate danger or fight off the attacker. Parallels for leadership are clear.

At night the sheep, sometimes two or three flocks together, would be herded into a sheep pen usually made up of loose stones built into low walls. There would be no gate or fence, consequently the shepherd would sleep across the entrance himself. In the mornings the shepherds would call their own sheep and the large flock would divide. From this we get the origin of sayings about the sheep knowing and being known by their shepherd, of hearing and trusting his voice, and of Jesus being the gate of the sheepfold (John Chapter 10).

There are other key passages where this shepherd image is found: Ezekiel 34.1–6, Zechariah 11.15–17, Jeremiah 31.10, 50.6 and Psalm 23. The task of the 'good' shepherd was to:

- have oversight of all the sheep;
- strengthen the weak and protect the lambs;
- care for the injured;
- search for the lost and bring back those who were straying;
- bring the sheep back into a united flock when they had become scattered;
- lead them on to good pastures for grazing;
- protect the flock from wild animals;
- guard at times of rest;
- regroup the flock for the next journey.

In contrast there are passages in Jeremiah and in Ezekiel condemning shepherds when they fail (Jeremiah 10.21, 12.10, 13.20, 22.22, 23.1, 2, 25.34–36, 49.19 and 50.6, 'Their shepherds have led them astray and caused them to roam'; Ezekiel 34.2–16, 'My flock lacks a shepherd and so has been plundered').

In the Old Testament there are also references to God as shepherd. The most familiar of these is in Psalm 23, 'The Lord is my shepherd, He will make me lie down in green pastures.' Across many other books there are references to the sheep as God's. In some places there are pointers to a future time when God will send another kind of shepherd, who will also be a king. Passages in Ezekiel 34.23 and Micah 5.5 are picked up in John 10 and a passage in Zechariah 13.7, 'Strike the shepherd and the sheep will be scattered' is used by Matthew in 26.31 and Mark at 14.27.

Jesus was himself aware of the shepherd-sheep analogy when describing himself and his ministry. Primarily in John 10 there is an outworking of the shepherd image as seen by him and a whole section of the Early Church. Here the good shepherd knows his sheep and the sheep recognize him as someone they can trust. The good shepherd is prepared to defend the sheep against attackers and will lay down his life for the sheep. In Hebrews 13.20 Jesus is described as the great shepherd of the sheep. Looking towards the second coming, the First Letter of Peter (5.4) talks about the time when the chief shepherd will appear.

In the Early Church those who became leaders were also described as shepherds. There are a number of references which are not just mentions but which come at pivotal and strategic points in the development of the church. In John 21.15–17 Jesus gives the charge to Peter 'Take care of my sheep'. Paul's farewell talk to the Ephesian elders in Acts 20.28, 29 commends them to 'Be shepherds of the church of God'.

Both Peter and Paul use the image of shepherd. Paul's teaching to the Christians in Ephesus was for some to act as pastors and for others to be apostle, prophet, evangelist and teacher. The first letter of Peter (2.25) gives theological weight to the image of sacrifice and of shepherding, 'By his wounds you have been healed. You were straying like sheep, but now you have turned towards the shepherd and guardian of your souls.'

The ministry of oversight of a group of people or a congregation comes as a strong concept in Peter's own teaching. In his same first letter (5.24) he says 'Be shepherds of God's flock . . . serving as overseers'. This has immediate resonances when we look, as in other parts of this book, at ideas of episcope or oversight which are much more inclusive and which could stand the weight of much collaborative reinterpretation.

The strength of the shepherd concept in leadership is that there are immediate connections for those who are in exposed positions of leadership today. The ideas universally linked with the responsibilities of any shepherd – of finding a way forward, of guidance and of protection – are there, as are the stressful experiences which come from taking calculated risks in order to guide and defend.[2]

## Prophet

Prophets were leaders in a different way. They were more like the 'thought' leaders or 'social' leaders I describe in Chapter 2 when

I distinguish between different types of leadership. The prophet led by being a disturber. Many prophets gained their authority as 'thought' leaders by being able to interpret a complex or frustrating situation in their own distinctive ways. They could condemn actions of contemporary leaders, kings or occupying powers but they did not leave it at that. They could see a solution, a way through, which would give hope to an oppressed or confused people. Often their words as 'social' leaders were accompanied by a symbolic gesture of the kind which intuitive leaders know is important for its visual impact and for its symbolism.

Prophets were the keepers of a king's conscience. Nathan was the prophet who condemned King David for engineering the death of Uriah the Hittite so that he could get Bathsheba for his own wife (2 Samuel, 11 and 12). Elijah condemned King Ahab for allowing Jezebel to engineer the murder of Naboth so that he could gain an extra piece of land (1 Kings 21). In these and other stories prophets led in very modern ways by saying that those in authority must not use their position to ride roughshod over basic human rights.

Prophets knew how to choose the right picture to illustrate a point. Amos looked at a basket of ripe fruit – in Hebrew the words for summer fruit and end are very similar – and foretold the end which might be awaiting Israel. In the same chapter 7 he drew images of locusts coming to devour a ripe crop, of a craftsman holding a plumb line against a building and of a people waiting for the new moon to be over so that they could sell their goods. All these were warnings of the consequences of actions motivated by greed or self-satisfaction. We Christians are familiar with significant symbolic acts and statements in our own history, from Martin Luther nailing his 95 Theses to the doors of the Castle Church in Wittenberg to Martin Luther King speaking prophetically, 'I have a dream that one day . . .'

Prophets also knew how to use symbolic examples. Hosea told a story about a man who took an unfaithful woman as his wife as a vivid illustration of God's relationship with a people who went after other gods (Hosea 1.2–11). Jeremiah bought a field at Anathoth, which was the family inheritance, to act as a symbol and pledge that a dispossessed people would one day return and possess their lands (Jeremiah 32.8–15).

Jeremiah showed that prophets were sometimes anxious that their interpretations and prophecies would be proved wrong. In chapter 1.11, at the very beginning of his work of prophecy, he noticed the blossom on a twig of an almond tree and wondered if one day he would be put to shame because what he said would not come to pass, or not bear fruit. As his prophecy matures in the use of imaginative symbolism Jeremiah describes how God led him to a potter's house and saw how the clay was being worked (Jeremiah 18). Whenever the vessel on which the potter was working became spoiled, it was changed into another vessel, such as seemed suitable in the potter's eyes. From this he drew the powerful illustration of how God could shape and reshape a people as the design for them developed. There is an interesting parallel here for our debate about the place of leadership in shaping and reshaping a church and, within that, for the developing of vocation and leadership in new ways if an original pattern is not working.

The prophet is not a leader who has direct responsibility for a people. This method of leadership gains its authority from the person speaking and acting with integrity. They are listened to and their words are acted on because their lives give credibility to the message they are giving.[3]

## Servant

The image of leadership through service was one on which Jesus drew for his ministry. It appears that he took the idea from the prophecies of Isaiah more than anywhere else. St John saw Jesus as a sacrificial lamb and altered the sequence of events at his trial to represent the imagery. In developing theories of leadership in modern times a model of servant is one of those which have found the most favour. The influential teachers and writers on leadership of the last generation, Stephen Covey and Robert Greenleaf, both have servant leadership as a main theme for their ideas.

It was part of the genius of Jesus that he developed the key passages in Isaiah to see how his life could be modelled on them. The word 'servant', *ebed* in Hebrew, occurs 800 times in the Old Testament and means worker. In biblical times servants were usually slaves, the property of their master or king. In ancient Israel the condition of a slave/servant was not necessarily demeaning. A slave might hold positions of trust and responsibility as Eliezer did for Abraham (Genesis 15.2) and, more well known, as Joseph did in Egypt. All subjects of a king are his servants and we can easily see how this kind of biblical language was used of everyone's relationship with God. Abraham (Genesis 26.24), Moses (Exodus 14.31) and David (2 Samuel 3.18) are among the most distinguished who are equally called 'servants' of God.

In the book of Isaiah there are four passages (42.1–4, 49.1–6, 50.4–9, 52.13–53.12) which take considerably further the concept of the 'servant of the Lord'. In these 'servant' poems the servant is the one who fulfils God's divine mission, which is not only to Israel but to the whole world. Here the servant, through suffering and death borne for the sins of others in a sacrificial way, rises from death and is exalted by God. The consequence of this is that those who had rejected him see the error of their ways and recognize that it was this sacrifice which gave them their salvation.

St Paul makes much of this sacrificial servant theme in his teaching and guidance to the Early Church. He insists that the significance of Christ's death on the cross is that he paid a price and delivered freedom from slavery for all who believe in him (1 Corinthians 6.20, 7.23). Believers are no longer slaves but children of God (Galatians 4.7). This comes with a warning, especially for leaders, that they should not become slaves to others (1 Corinthians 7.23).

*Servant leadership* is an approach to leadership development, coined and defined by Robert Greenleaf and advanced by several authors such as Stephen Covey, Peter Block, Peter Senge, and others. Servant leadership emphasizes the leader's role as *steward* of the resources, human, financial and otherwise provided by an organization. It encourages leaders to serve others while staying focused on achieving results in line with the organization's values and integrity.

The modern concept of servant leadership started with Robert Greenleaf, who published his essay, 'The Servant as Leader', in 1970.[4] This led to further essays from Greenleaf, and further works from others, in recent years. However, the concept is thousands of years older than this and stems, at least partly as we know, from Jesus' teachings on leadership. Servant leadership differs from other leadership approaches by eschewing the common top-down hierarchical style, and instead emphasizes collaboration, trust, empathy, and the ethical use of power. At heart, the individual is a servant first, making the conscious decision to lead. His drive is to lead because he wants to serve better, not because he desires increased power. The objective is to enhance the growth of individuals in the organization and increase teamwork and personal involvement.

Greenleaf says:

The servant leader is the servant first . . . It begins with the natural feeling that one wants to serve, to serve first. Then conscious choice brings one to aspire to lead. He or she is sharply different from the person who is leader first.[5]

Larry Spears, the current director of the Greenleaf Centre, has described servant leadership in this way:

As we near the end of the twentieth century, we are beginning to see that traditional autocratic and hierarchical models of leadership are slowly yielding to a newer model – one that attempts simultaneously to embrace the personal growth of workers and improve the quality and caring of our many institutions through a combination of teamwork and community, personal involvement and decision-making, and ethical caring behaviour. This emerging approach to leadership and service is called *Servant Leadership*.[6]

## us as leader and team builder

In a particularly stimulating Grove Booklet, Peter Shaw, who is a management coach and experienced consultant, has set out six leadership characteristics of Jesus.[7] He also includes the concept of servant. The strength and delight of his booklet is that he is able to make strong and recognizable links between his business experience and the New Testament tradition. His introduction sets out the dilemmas which face leaders today. These include the need to define the clearest possible strategy, to set priorities amid a sea of demands, ensuring there is space to reflect, the need to communicate effectively and succinctly and the like. He looks at the key characteristics of Jesus as leader under six themes: Jesus as visionary, servant leader, teacher, coach, radical and healer.

As a visionary, Jesus did not meander aimlessly, he had a strong sense of purpose. As a servant, Shaw says, Jesus did not display servitude but a generosity of spirit. As a teacher, Jesus' aim was for his hearers to grow in wisdom and understanding. I like best of all the splendid aphorism of Shaw's about Jesus as coach. He says, 'He built his own team, but they were not people in his own mould.' This example alone, if developed, would enable many of our leaders to achieve more and get the very best in support and advice from those around them – frustrating as working with different types of people certainly can be! It is comforting and salutary to remember after a bad staff, team or board meeting that Jesus has been there before us!

During his entire public ministry Jesus chose and then mentored a small group of men and women. Shaw points out particularly that, although the disciples and followers were from his own culture, they came from different backgrounds. He worked hard through severe frustrations to build them into a team. As he travelled and confronted many different people he put them all in challenging situations. He took the risk of chancing how imperfectly they had understood his message when he sent them out in twos. In doing this he expected the disciples to develop their own understanding of his vision and to articulate it.

The full benefit of his coaching became clear only after his resurrection and ascension. He had worked with them throughout the months and years of his ministry. It was only after he had gone from them that the formation they had received gave them enough inner strength to begin a mission which became both a church and an international movement.

Shaw reflects on the leadership style of Jesus. He says that good leaders have always spent one-to-one time with their immediate staff. Jesus spent a lot of time coaching his top team. He was tough with them, often speaking strong words and expressing exasperation at their slowness in understanding. The role of leader as coach means the use of both hard and soft skills to get the best out of the team. In a wise comment, echoing John Adair, Shaw points out that both individual and team skills have to be developed if effectiveness is to be achieved in carrying out the task.

Shaw also gives us Jesus as a radical leader. Here he sees Jesus as someone who knew and understood the traditions, the history and rules of his nation and religion but who was not afraid to break the mould. He reminds us that this ministry was carried out after times of reflection. Jesus as healer, he says, is less like the modern business leader. I am not so sure. Much good leadership is about creation and recreation, about redeeming broken or fallen situations. Good leaders bring healing and a sense of well-being, and for the right reasons.

The example of Jesus as leader is one which is central to vocation and devotion as well as an inspiration for good leadership today. Jesus stands as one of the great figures in the history of the world. What he said and did should not be confined only to religious modelling. His life, example, sayings and significance as a leader need to be understood as placing him among the greatest strategists and team builders the world has ever seen.

## The leadership of St Paul

Paul faced a different challenge. He was involved with a dispersed community of disciples, believers and converts and knew that he had to play a major part in establishing and harmonizing the character of the new Christian communities. Paul was a theoretical and systematic thinker, again a different kind of leader. He used his letters to teach and to influence. He came up with the most developed thinking about the purpose and significance of Jesus' life and God's purposes in it and after it.

As a significant and influential leader he knew that he needed to come up with an image and concept which would unite believers around a common theme. He gave the scattered communities of Christians a harmonizing imagery, that of being members, individually and corporately, of the Body of Christ. In 1 Corinthians 12.12–31 he speaks in terms of a body which is a living unit by virtue of its various limbs and organs, each with their own particular function. The belonging is local but by developing this mind-picture a wider corporate identity, located in beliefs and values which were to become universal, became a theological way of understanding how churches become the Church. By doing this Paul was setting out a template which exists to this day and one which expresses the creative tension between local identity and autonomy and any universal belief and structure which binds the world-wide Christian community together in one family and communion. It is an identity which comes to the surface and is called into question each time a deep controversy emerges. The task of senior leaders and their teams is to restate the basic concepts and attempt to hold the whole family together. No one pretends this is easy. Sometimes these attempts have been successful but on other occasions they have led to divisions and even to new movements and denominations.

## A never ending story

In looking at images of leadership in the Bible my problem is where to stop. The portrait gallery can go on and on. Leadership in the Bible as a concept can fill many books and I hope that it will continue to do so! New aspects of leadership can be seen by each generation as they visit and revisit this rich and diverse book. Whenever new secular theories emerge, many or most can be described as being foreshadowed in some part or other of the Bible. I hope that the ways in which leadership has been described with these major examples will give a sufficient appetite for biblical concepts of leadership and the people behind them to be quarried more and more. The need for well-resourced and reflective leadership done by biblically inspired people is central for the leadership of a God-centred Church.

## Notes

1. Lawrence Nevard, *Management and Vision in the Church*. Leadership Development Group Publication, *c.*1972. Much of what is included in this chapter has been prompted by my re-reading the papers entrusted to my care when the Leadership Development Group decided to close its activities.
2. A full exploration of the use of the concept of shepherd as leaders has been done by John Truscott. His article 'The leader as a shepherd' and other papers can be downloaded from his website at www. john-truscott.co.uk.
3. For an extended description of the methods used by prophets see J. Lindblom, *Prophecy in Ancient Israel*, Blackwell, Oxford, 1967 and later editions.
4. Robert K. Greenleaf, *Servant Leadership*, Paulist Press, 1997. See also Stephen R. Covey, *The Seven Habits of Highly Effective People*, Simon and Schuster, 1992, and *The 8th Habit: From Effectiveness to Greatness*, Simon and Schuster, 2001.
5. Robert K. Greenleaf, *The Servant as Leader*, 1970. See www. greenleaf.org.
6. Larry Spears, *Reflections on Leadership*, 1995. See www.greenleaf. org.
7. Peter Shaw, *Mirroring Jesus as Leader*, Grove Books Ethics Series No E 135, 2004.

# 6

# What's New in New-Shape Church?

When hasn't there been newness in shapes of church? Every phase in the history and life of our churches has had pressure groups, experiments and factions which threaten to break away and create new churches or denominations. The shape of our churches is determined by such movements. Luther, Calvin, the Wesleys; Baptists, Presbyterians, Congregationalists, Quakers all represent names and groups, movements and denominations within the history of our churches. They reflect faith and tradition in many mirrors. The Reformation gave birth to Anglicanism in a form which has changed and adapted from the Elizabethan Settlement to the world-wide variety it has today. The Universal Catholic Church became the Roman Catholic and Orthodox Church in East and West in order to define itself against new movements and fundamental divisions. Where do we go next and which new shapes should be encouraged to emerge?

There is a saying attributed to Albert Einstein about the need for new ideas and the place of some of them in the scheme of things: 'We have to develop new ideas to solve the problems which were created by the new ideas of the previous generation.' Even if that remark is a little over-cynical there is a grain of truth in it. We can all attest to the experience of new church leaders being appointed and coming in with a range of new ideas to solve the problems as they see them. Some even describe these as caused by the way things were done in the past. Politicians regularly blame the problems they have to deal with on the policies of the previous party in power. Many congregations and groups of local churches get wearied by new programmes and plans which break on them with increasing frequency. I have seen some parish profiles which ask for the next appointment not to be someone who will lead in that way. The real task and challenge for leaders and leadership teams is to know when to begin a process of change and which programmes and ideas to use to achieve their agreed aims.

The word *enigma* belongs not only to a cleverly encrypted code for transmitting messages in World War Two. It is a Greek word used only once in the New Testament in 1 Corinthians 13.12 and contrasts present and future seeing. This early Bible study by St Paul uses two words with tantalizing significance for our exploration of new shapes of church. What he says, in a literal translation, is 'we see through a mirror a riddle' and in a more familiar translation 'now we see through a glass only darkly'. He uses the word $εινιγμά$ which means a puzzle, riddle or even a paradox. Paul is connecting with its use in Numbers 12.8 where God speaks to his prophets, except Moses, in riddles. These riddles are put alongside visions in Numbers 12.6. The word here is $έσοπτρον$ which means to see a reflection in a glass. The rabbis speak of the prophets seeing God in nine clouded mirrors. Paul is bringing into our exploration of leadership a profound piece of rabbinic exegesis. The experienced leader sees in present events reflections of what has gone before and in this a series of choices, some paradoxical or contradictory about where to go next. The Church as it is can give birth to a series of possible new shapes. The leader has to discern which to encourage and support. It is rarely clear what to do next. Wisdom in leadership emerges by balancing a whole range of decisions and by trying to solve the 'riddle' of what to do next.

## One new shape or many?

The enigma or riddle facing all church leaders is how many recognizable shapes of church there can be. At its most extreme it is quite possible to say that there is one Church of God which encompasses all those in the trinitarian 'family' of denominations. At the other extreme it is just as possible to say that there is no one expression of church which all can recognize but that belief is reflected in a whole series of movements each of which have glimpsed part of the revelation of God in their age and time.

Unfortunately neither of these extremes will do as real and accurate descriptions of church. There have to be some 'boundaries' by which a kind of orthodoxy is recognized and accepted by the Christian traditions which have given birth to major national and international churches. It is not possible, and should not be possible, for one group or one person to claim all of the truth for any age. Yet we have the paradox of denominations, now venerable in their wisdom, which have been founded in just such a way. The shape of the Church of the future will have to absorb and accommodate difference as well as development. No doubt some time will have to be given to putting right the mistakes of the past in order to move on or to end the bright ideas of a previous generation.

What is happening in Britain as in many other parts of the world is that green shoots of new life are emerging to express faith and belief outside the normal patterns of congregational culture and worship. Many of these reach people who would not normally come to a church or join a congregation which meets every Sunday morning. These new shapes or fresh expressions of community and of worship are taking many forms. They range from a 'café church', where people sit around tables and discuss and pray, to meetings in schools and public halls. There are events which attract young people and worship events which accompany the elderly at that particular stage in their life. Almost all have an evangelistic, faith-sharing element to them and are motivated by the knowledge that traditional forms of church and of worship will only reach and attract a small section of any population.

My reasons for wanting to place contemporary changes and divisions in perspective is that, for the past 150 or more years, denominations have been struggling to come to terms with accelerated change and there are lessons to be learned. Changes which have created the life of congregations as we know them began with industrialization, which led to or forced great movements of the population of Europe to cities or to become emigrants to other parts of the world. It continued through the experience of two world wars and many other devastating international events. Society has had to come to terms with the Holocaust and the fact of atomic warfare and now with extremist terror organizations fuelled by faith. Theologians in the 1960s and 1970s, not very long ago, could write about 'religionless Christianity', philosophers spoke about the 'death' of God and sociologists of religion about secularization and the components which lead to the erosion of belief. So much has happened since then that it is hard to know where our modern 'new shape' church begins. In the West and in England in particular we now have a situation where those attending house churches or non-denominational churches in schools and warehouse-like buildings rival the numbers and vibrancy of those who attend even lively churches in the mainstream denominations. The shape of the Church is indeed changing – and being led – in challenging new ways.

Let's look at some of the new shapes the churches have taken in the Western world since the processes of industrialization and urbanization began. These examples reflect images of changes in leadership which are taking place today and will assist our own processes of reflective practice – or the solving of riddles. Much of my ministry over the past 35 years has been a part of these movements with their history and later developments. I hope that these snapshot stories will give us a distance and objectivity which will help us in much of our present practice of ministry when we are asked to encourage a range of new shapes of church and new patterns for worship.

I have another reason for not writing about only immediate new movements in church life. It is that others are doing this more comprehensively and with better information than I have. Steven Croft and his colleagues in Fresh Expressions are engaged in this work and will publish their evidence in their own ways. Information can be found at their website www.freshexpressions.org.uk. These are reinforced by the recently published work about patterns of churchgoing from Peter Brierley and Christian Research. What they produce will place immediate changes in their context. Mine is a contribution of perspective. As someone who has been part of the 'new shapes' which are now our immediate history I can at least say that I was there and know what it felt like at the time. As a student I worked in Boston, USA, alongside Harvey Cox, the author of the iconic book *Secular City*.[1] I have been chaplain and then senior chaplain in the Sheffield Industrial Mission, perhaps the best-known fresh expression of outreach and identification in the church world of its day. This new shape of church with a distinctive leadership grew from the attempts of worker priests and others to 'identify' with people in their work environment. I was, I think, the first to write in a theological journal about a new spirituality and 'the death of secular man'.[2] I have been a part of an international ecumenical educational network which has pioneered new methods of learning and of adult education. We have developed the strong belief that an informed and vibrant core of believers exercising 'lay discipleship' is the most significant call from God to any changing society and emerging new-shape church. One of the most significant books about adult learning from this generation had a fitting title: *Tomorrow is Another Country*.[3]

I was once a speaker at an international conference on the Adult Catechumenate. The other speaker was much more interesting, especially because he gave us a symbolic picture. It resembled an Ascension scene painted in the apse of a church. But instead of the risen Christ's hand being raised in a blessing he seemed to have a twisted or broken wrist. My speaker colleague said this gesture could be of enormous significance for a church trying to change. In this picture from a church in Spain, I cannot remember where, the risen Christ was calling his followers *from the future* towards the church and society which they could create. That picture and its image has stayed with me ever since. It is the picture I hope you will have in your mind as we explore what Christ's followers in recent generations have tried to do as they listened and then acted on their call from the future to leadership in the present.

## The Navvy Mission

The most interesting and influential of those strident and emerging lay people to begin to forge new shapes for the church was a woman, Mrs Elizabeth Garnett, who was the leading organizer and writer for the Navvy Mission, formed in 1878 after a long history of informal activity. From the beginning of the canal-building era to the end of the laying of railway tracks gangs of migrant workers had moved from construction site to construction site across Britain. They belonged to no one's parish in the recognizable way in which English religion had been organized since the Middle Ages. The industrial process of building the communications infrastructure for the industrial age took no account of settled communities and rurally determined boundaries. Mrs Garnett organized an interdenominational association of preachers and evangelists, ordained and lay, to minister to these itinerant groups of construction workers. Temporary chapels were built for worship and the performing of baptisms, marriages and funerals. Terry Coleman in his book *The Railway Navvies* has, to our ears, bizarre stories of bodies of fatally injured navvies being moved across parish boundaries to avoid the complexities of their burial. When I went to work in South Yorkshire in the late 1960s the term 'over the brush' was still used for couples who were living together without an official marriage ceremony. In the navvy camps, without organized religion, a couple would jump over a broomstick to symbolize their union.[4]

The Navvy Mission attempted to work with these dispossessed and unchurched people. Attempts at welfare were many and the missioners, in this first 'new-shape' church, became highly respected for their caring activities. In the journal of the Mission called *The Quarterly Letter to Navvies* Mrs Garnett and her colleagues wrote evangelistic and moral exhortations. These were no doubt heeded by some. What was most valued by those who could not read, as well as by those who could, was the back page. Here were listed all those navvies who had been killed or injured as well as the places where the new works were going to be. The Navvy Mission combined evangelistic outreach with social care in ways which would have been as easily recognizable by the early church and the religious orders of the Middle Ages as it is in the service and mission of the new-shape churches of today. It was done in a new way to meet new needs. What is significant is that this movement was one of the first to recognize that new patterns of society would need new methods of contacting great sections of the population of a country.

These new movements would still go alongside more 'traditional' methods associated with leadership in an inherited or traditional church. New buildings were the principal method of outreach for all denominations. The Methodist revival of the late eighteenth century had seen the beginning of the establishment of new, and simpler, buildings for Nonconformist worship. The local ownership and fundraising associated with these made them a new shape of church. The national census of 1851 contained a question about religious allegiance. For the Church of England this spelled out the need to provide more buildings and more seats, free seats, in urban areas and new towns. Thus began an enormous programme of church building for the next 50 years. Many fine pieces of architecture were created as some of the best architects, artists and craftsmen created buildings primarily in the shape and form of the Gothic Revival.

Professor Robin Gill[5] has pointed out that this burst of building continued past the time of increases in church attendance. Many of the largest buildings were completed at a time when they could never be filled week by week. Thus the sense that buildings were more half empty than nearly full began to demoralize many local congregations. Gill also points out that the cost of some of these ambitious buildings placed an additional burden on declining congregations at a time when reserves of energy and cash might have been better spent on gospel sharing and social outreach. In this case a programme for expansion and development was being led by local and national leaders who were either unable or unwilling to accept changes which were already taking place.

## New-shape leaders

At the same time in the late nineteenth and early twentieth centuries a new kind of ecclesiastical leadership and presence was emerging across the denominations. Many with a sense of historical perspective will be familiar with the concept that early trade union leaders learned their public oratory and local organizing skills through the emerging Nonconformist churches, especially those associated with the various forms of Methodism.

Equally significant was a turning towards the need to address major public and employment issues by academics, some of whom were church leaders. Christian evangelicalism had already produced lay leaders such as William Wilberforce (1799–1833), who had worked so tirelessly for the abolition of slavery, and Lord Shaftesbury (1801–89), who had taken important Acts of social and factory reform through parliament. Now church leaders themselves were getting involved.

Cardinal Manning offered to intervene in the Docker's Strike of 1889 and was held in great respect for his actions. Of greater interest and perhaps of more lasting significance was the social concern of significant educationalists and church leaders who were, in some ways, 'on the edge' of the establishment. John Malcolm Ludlow, Charles Kingsley, Frederick Denison Maurice, Thomas Hughes and their associates between the years 1848 and 1854 formed a group called the Christian Socialists. They were not socialists as we came to know them in the twentieth century but they did begin to think in very public ways about the competitive, acquisitive nature of their society which had become rich through trade and empire. Maurice wrote to Charles Kingsley, author of *The Water Babies*, 'competition is put forth as a law of the universe. That is a lie. The time has come for us to declare that it is a lie by word and by deed.' Maurice claimed that the true law of the universe was that humankind was created to live in community. He said, 'people realise their true nature when they co-operate with one another as children of God and brothers and sisters in Christ'. These views were echoed in a significant way in the Papal Encyclical *Rerum Novarum* in 1891 where, among many other things, the workplace was described as a social community.

The most public Anglican development which went alongside the work of the Navvy Mission was that of the Christian Social Union. Henry Scott Holland was a Canon of St Paul's Cathedral in London and later became Regius Professor of Divinity in the University of Oxford. As a writer and thought leader of his 'new-shape church', he spoke out against social and economic evils and lobbied for their rectification. The Christian Social Union campaigned for factory reform, produced pamphlets and held public meetings. In 1919 it was merged with the Navvy Mission to become the Industrial Christian Fellowship (ICF). This campaigning, evangelistic and reforming organization had as its Missioner Geoffrey Studdert Kennedy (Woodbine Willie), the best known of the World War One army chaplains. William Temple, later Archbishop of Canterbury, was one of its active speakers. Throughout the 1930s and in World War Two, with its conferences on social and political issues, the ICF continued to place the thinking of the churches at the forefront of social action. Its post-war flowering was in the worker priest movement in France and the Industrial Mission chaplaincies which flourished across Britain. This new shape thinking had particular and influential consequences. Their prophetic stance, however, has almost completely excluded them from the active work of the churches.[6]

In 1926 R. H. Tawney, a lifelong friend and associate of Temple, produced a major critique of capitalist society in *Religion and the Rise of Capitalism*.[7] As a vision for the reconstruction of Britain after World War Two, Temple himself produced *Christianity and Social Order*, a booklet which lived on and was republished with a preface by Edward Heath as recently as 1976. The thinking and influence of this group of people gave some of the shape to post-war reforms in governments of more than one political colour. As Archbishop Temple commented at the beginning of *Christianity and Social Order*, not all prophecy and ecclesiastical intervention was welcomed. When the Bench of Anglican Bishops offered to intervene and mediate in the coal strike of 1926 they were given a robust rebuke. Mr Baldwin, Prime Minister and coal owner, said this intervention was as unwelcome as the industrialists and unions involved offering to rewrite the Athanasian Creed!

It is these roots of a different kind of leadership in the churches which have formed and informed much of the public action of the churches in the twentieth century. Leaders were quite as concerned with righting social wrongs as they were with church reform, because their focus was the Kingdom of God and its immediate possibilities in the world. I have given some of them a brief re-airing here, not to tell an old story again, but to demonstrate that Christian leadership does not just 'pop-up' with able individuals who can work a synodical system or who are good with media and public addresses. Leadership of this kind was nurtured through generations of thought and social concern. It had a significant intellectual content. Its attractiveness was sufficient to encourage people of considerable ability to offer themselves in the service of the churches. Its later fruit was seen as much as anywhere in the Christian Action grouping which produced *Faith in the City*[8] and the social action associated with the Church Urban Fund, which I shall describe in Chapter 7.

## Ecumenism

My generation has seen two distinct internal, inter-church movements which now define the 'new shape' of our churches. The first has been the great urge to bring the historic denominations closer together. The other has been an increase in divisions arising from irreconcilable views of Scripture and ethics. Beginning with an initiative which emerged from the Edinburgh Missionary Conference of 1912, there has been a general will for denominations to come closer together, and for some to merge. The movement was encouraged in a great way when Cardinal Basil Hume brought the Roman Catholic Church more fully into its proceedings at a conference at Swanwick in 1997. The irony of this landmark piece of ecumenical commitment is that it came only just before a time when international divisions within Christianity were being accelerated by member churches which have grown to independence from that same missionary movement.

Sandwiched between these two events is a segment in the history of our churches which has given shape to more inter-national church leadership than ever before. Those who have participated could claim the title of statesmen and stateswomen. Beginning in the 1920s, and probably in the decades before in different ways, scholars and church leaders across Western Europe began to meet together. It is certainly true that scholar-ship has always been international. For the study of theology this international movement began with strong links between German, Scandinavian and British theologians from 1870 onwards and led to succeeding scholars who became church leaders developing a strong international European bond. What is most significant is that this international solidarity was held throughout World War Two by such international statespeople as Archbishop William Temple, Bishop George Bell, the Revd Dr Visser t'Hooft and the Swedish Archbishop Nathan Söderblom. Their leadership became visionary in their meetings and writing about how Europe might be recreated when peace came and in the way in which a 'new-shape' ecumenical federation of churches might be created. This latter became the World Council of Churches with its international headquarters in Geneva. Although mentioned as individuals these leaders were formed by colleagueship and networking across the Continent of Europe and beyond. Leadership and the nurture of a whole set of attitudes towards the future can develop when such conditions are created. This networking provides an interesting lesson for those who want to create attitudes to leadership which would bring consistent policies leading to lasting change.

## A divided new-shape Church

One of the most significant changes in the shape of our churches over the past 30 or less years is that they have sprung new divi-sions. These splits are seen most publicly and institutionally in the Church of England but are present in all the historic denominations and, in less explicit ways, in newly created churches and congregations. Some of these divisive questions also exist in other world faiths.

It is now possible to say, in a very loose and general sense but one which is strong and painful to many, that the divisions within international Christianity today are not between the old high church or Catholic denominations and groups and the low church or evangelical groups. They are between those who hold an open view of Scripture and its culturally related origins and those who hold a tight view of Scripture and the uniqueness and once-for-all nature of the views and revelations held in them. These two views are not simplistically to be called liberal and conservative. They contain too many sophisticated elements for that. I am sure that it is right not to polarize views in extremes at all. That would be an inaccurate description of what is happening to the churches at the moment. However, there is certainly a background or template with these approaches not only to Scripture but also to society and learning in general which has led to some of our new tensions. Tomorrow's leaders will have to work in the context of these differences while themselves being formed in one or other of these traditions.

The Church of England has created a new character for itself over the way in which it chose to deal with the debate about the ordination of women to the priesthood and to the historic episcopate. This is not a place to look again at the story of that debate, or at its theology. It is the place to look at what new shapes of leadership emerged during and after the debate and at the way in which 'seeing a riddle through a mirror' leadership enabled a difficult forward step to be taken.

## MOW

The movement entitled MOW – the Movement for the Ordination of Women – produced a new generation of women, with many men also, who came to the fore as leaders of a movement whose time had come by the early 1980s. What is interesting in terms of leadership is that many of these people had been working and preparing a culture so that the receptive moment could be grasped when it came. Leadership can be given by ideas and influence discreetly in the background and is well demonstrated in the work of MOW. Many or most of its leaders did not want themselves to become leaders in the hierarchy of the Church of England. They became leaders for a time, concentrating on a single issue. With the narrowest of margins at a General Synod vote in 1993, the advocates achieved their aim. Leadership of this type brought into vocal prominence people of great ability who had been influential in the background of our churches for many years.

The organization of a campaign took huge resources and provoked emotive responses quite as powerful as the strong arguments used to substantiate the movement. Within the leadership of the Church of England was the challenge of how to manage an issue which was potentially so divisive. It was inevitable that there would be 'winners and losers' but how could a split in the denomination be avoided? What emerged was a new interpretation of unity by which quite differing groups could be held together. The idea of 'two integrities' was born so that opposing groups could remain within a united concept and understanding of the Church of England. It is still an open debate as to how much this was viewed as a transitional situation or as one which would become permanent.

## Forward in Faith

The opposing groups agreed on a compromise settlement containing an acceptance of the two integrities as a way forward. Many understood that this agreement was provisional in order to respect the consciences of those who disagreed. However, leaders who emerged in the opposition movement called Forward in Faith saw that it was likely to become more permanent. A protracted stand-off was needed because of the strident and authoritative leadership of those who wanted to remain Anglican but who could not accept women as priests or as bishops. The arguments against were pragmatic and contained ecumenical sensitivities. This meant that, in the 'through a glass darkly' sense, there might at some time in the future be a Council or the like when the Eastern and Western Catholic Churches revised their position. Leaders of Forward in Faith, which had a strong lay male and female as well as clerical element, found themselves catapulted into new structural positions of leadership. Like those in MOW, many were to have prominence just for the issues and its compromise resolution but others in both 'integrities' had to learn new leadership skills. They became hierarchical leaders in an inclusive church which required them to relate to all the members of that church and not just to those who shared their views. The dilemma continues for them and affects us all, particularly with regard to our ecumenical relationships.

## Leadership in a new-shape divided church

There are enormous new lessons to be learned regarding leadership in churches with severe fractures and divisions. Denominations approach these in different ways. Methodism is held together with the concept of 'connexion' which means much to the members and has something of the connotations of 'family', implying a belonging to one another stronger than anything any one member does to sever them. The Roman Catholic Church has, or so it seems to me, its own unacknowledged stance to difference. Papal encyclicals and letters state a position which church leaders can then reinforce in their public statements. This is all done in the context of a clear knowledge that many members choose to ignore or disobey these commands. Some public acts of disobedience place members outside their church. Many other divisive issues are not brought into the open and leaders with their members live in this uneasy truce as laws and decrees change and develop.

The Church of England has placed itself in a more difficult situation insofar as it has chosen to institutionalize its differences. For leaders this creates extra tensions within a denomination trying to move on and develop new missionary shapes. Many leaders have been promoted because they reflect one of the differences in the church. When forming part of a senior staff team significant questions arise. The 'team' has been formed not to bring in complementary skills but to reflect difference. If the hope is that a bishop and his team reflect episcope and gain their authority to lead because they represent a focus for unity, this position is demonstrably hard to maintain.

This rift has different consequences in different parts of the international Anglican communion. The whole 'family' of dioceses and provinces holds itself together in the acceptance of another concept word, that of 'communion'. Cynics now wonder if it will, in the future, be possible to speak of the Anglican Communion. The concept is a little like that used after the ending of the British Empire – members regrouped themselves as the British Commonwealth with the monarch as the head. Many tensions have challenged the Anglican family. We anticipate with great interest the events of the 2008 Lambeth Conference of all bishops in the Anglican Communion and wait to see how the representative leader, the Archbishop of Canterbury, holds the family together as he reinterprets his authority and redefines its influence.

## Catechumenate and Emmaus

For the majority of Christians not involved in ecclesiastical politics the growth and development of their local church is what comes top of their list of priorities. They want to know what leadership is emerging and how an increased interest in spirituality can connect with the activities of their local communities. For the past 40 years, in response to those who are enquiring about faith there has been a significant development of new shapes of church. The decline in numbers of priests in mission situations has resulted in the use of catechists across the world, especially in Africa. Their method of teaching and faith-sharing was taken up and recommended for wide use by the Second Vatican Council (1962–5). In developing a method of learning, the Catechumenate linked the teaching, initiation methods and ceremonies of the Early Church with modern educational teaching and faith-sharing methods.

The Catechumenate is not only a Roman Catholic method of faith sharing and initiation. It has been taken up and adapted by the Episcopal Church in the United States, the Lutheran Church of Sweden and the Church of England. In this country Peter Ball and a group of associates pioneered this work and an account of it is given by Peter and myself in *Faith on the Way*.[9] The development of this work made a considerable contribution to the building up of confidence in lay people to explore their own faith with those who were enquiring about belief and who were on their way to joining a local congregation. The Church of England House of Bishops commended this comprehensive method of working in an unimplemented report called *On the Way*.[10] Catechumenal methods have renewed some parts of the inherited, traditional Church and have encouraged some of the patterns we now see in the new shapes of church.

In England the basic method of working used by advocates of the Catechumenate was experiential, beginning with the questions which enquirers were asking and journeying on from there. Nevertheless, many felt that such a way of working was not structured enough and that accompanying resource material was needed. The Emmaus course now provides this in a comprehensive way. Using a wide range of background and informative discussion materials the Emmaus course takes the catechumenal process on to another stage and has been widely used. Here a bottom-up leadership has begun to change the church.

## Alpha and Fresh Expressions

Far more widely used and more influential in creating new shapes of church life have been the Alpha courses and the movement which has grown from them. Most interesting for a study of leadership is that the whole international work of Alpha was not planned by a national church, synod or education board. It grew from work done locally at the church of Holy Trinity, Brompton for those who worked in London but who travelled to their other homes in the country for the weekends. Sharing a meal with teaching and discussion took off in astonishing ways. Material of a high quality for midweek group discussion and to support those meeting was and is still produced.

Not least in leading the development of Alpha has been the way in which Christian businesspeople saw that there was an enormous market for information about the Christian faith coupled with the building up of local fellowship or community groups. Well-presented and marketed videos and teaching materials found a ready audience in a changed situation where many were searching for somewhere to belong in a world where it is becoming increasingly hard to make friends and join groups. When this situation is coupled with the lack of communication between generations and the decline of education in the Christian faith Alpha came as a way of meeting many contemporary needs at the same time.

## Fresh Expressions of Church

The institutional churches have now come to realize that traditional methods of worship and inherited structures of support for local congregations are of little or no interest to young people or to other sections of society who are separated from active participation in the life of Christian communities. With this realization there is a sense in which we have now come full-circle in modern life from those early attempts to connect with separated communities by the Navvy Mission. The denominations have begun a number of 'mission' initiatives to make new connections. In the Church of England Archbishop George Carey and others initiated Springboard as a team of evangelists who would work with dioceses in their attempts to contact diverse groups. The Emmaus publications and study courses linked catechumenal processes with printed resources in ways which supported evangelistic enterprise.

No one answer can be offered which will connect faith with types of worship, even for particular generations. The new phrase 'Fresh Expressions of Church' has become the umbrella term which holds the new movements and experiments together. Its information gathering and experience demonstrates that new forms of worship and different ways of accompanying enquirers are likely to be quite localized and enormously varied. It is my hope that when more emerges from the work of Steve Croft and his team we shall be able to categorize which types of leadership are emerging and which are successful in their application. I have a strong hunch that we shall discover some very interesting and exciting pieces of leadership of much wider significance than any caricature of 'modern' Church with flashing lights and coffee-bar-style worship. We shall see clergy and laity deeply committed to the local expression of church, in the main committed to the work of building community.

## Vision and leadership in a new-shape church

There are more examples of new shapes of leadership bringing new life outside the churches than within them. Let me end with one which has in its story all the concepts of new life and resurrection that we would expect to see as churches change and adapt.

There is another Eden and it has given me a new vision of leadership. This astonishing new development is the Eden Project in Cornwall. Here a former china-clay quarry, destined for a second use as a rubbish tip for the town of St Austell, has been transformed into a series of gardens and greenhouse sub-climates by a visionary team of leaders. The visitor arrives at the project and in a very clear and accessible way is made aware of the aims of the project and the philosophy behind it.

Here is a major tourist attraction, prepared as a Millennium Project, which achieves an 'energy neutral' balance between what it takes out of the planet to run and what it puts back. Virtually all waste is recycled. The soil has been recreated from compost and every visitor is encouraged to replace their litter in appropriate containers. The opening sentences of the visitor booklet make the aims and the values clear:

> Between 1988 and 1996 a group of people gathered in pubs, hotels, private houses, offices and even motorway service

ations to talk about an idea. What idea? To create a place like
nothing anyone had seen before; a place that explored human
dependence on plants and the natural world; a place that might
just make a difference. It was ridiculous to imagine that
hundreds of people trained to say no could be persuaded to say
yes. But the greybeards had a plan: ask the youngsters to do it
– they don't know it can't be done.

What drives us? Well, cynicism doesn't seem to have made
the world a better place, so we thought we'd try innocence. We
chose the name Eden, not for religious reasons, but because
we liked the idea that, if Man was thrown out of paradise for
eating from the tree of knowledge, maybe the way to return
was to eat more of the same.

In this real life modern story we encounter clear vision, definitely
stated values, new life, responsible stewardship and inclusive
partnerships. If only each visitor to a church was able to understand the values and aims of the congregation in such a clear and
inviting way!

I went on my own visit to the Eden Project and was excited by
the impression it made on me. Later on my same visit to Cornwall
I discussed this visionary place with the Bishop of Truro and
his staff. The bishop said that he has sat in on a Project board
meeting. When different departments brought their demands and
development ideas to the table it would have been easy for competitiveness of a divisive kind to emerge. He said this was avoided
by the founder stopping the discussion and reminding the whole
'community' what their overall aims were and what values held
them together. The chair explained that they were not developing
a bigger and better ecological theme park, nor were they developing a massive education project or even a pretty series of
gardens for tourists. Once the direction had been restated and
agreed then fair and reasonable discussion continued.

Here is a model for new-shape church. The values which hold
us together need to be restated over and over again. The task of
leaders is to hold the vision and keep consensus around it. The
catechumenal task is to ensure that the values and beliefs of the

organization, our church, are transmitted before the enquirer leaves as 'just a tourist'. Many of our current 'new-shape' church projects build on the Eden experience of involving the kind of able young people who only know how to say yes and to search for possible ways forward. Those of us who have lived long enough to see our picture of new-shape church seem rather dated can learn that, under the God who calls us forward to a new future, exciting things are possible if a new generation of creative and innovative leaders can be identified and developed. We go on now to look at the many places from which leadership can come in churches of all shapes and sizes.

## Notes

1. Harvey Cox, *Secular City*, Macmillan, New York, 1966.
2. Thomas Altizer and William Hamilton, *The Death of God*, Bobbs-Merril, 1966, Paul Van Buren, *The Secular Meaning of the Gospel*, SCM Press, 1963.
3. Yvonne Craig (ed.), *Tomorrow is Another Country*, Church of England Board of Education, Church House Publishing, 1996.
4. Terry Coleman, *The Railway Navvies*, Pelican, 1968.
5. Robin Gill, *The Myth of the Empty Church*, SPCK, 1993.
6. John Mantle, *Britain's Worker Priests*, SCM Press, 2000.
7. R. H. Tawney, *Religion and the Rise of Capitalism*, John Murray, 1926, many subsequent reprints and as a Pelican book.
8. *Faith in the City, Report of the Archbishops' Commission into Urban Areas*, Church House Bookshop, 1984.
9. Peter Ball and Malcolm Grundy, *Faith on the Way*, Continuum, 2000.
10. *On the Way: Towards an Integrated Approach to Christian Initiation*, House of Bishops' report on the Catechumenate, Church House Publishing, 1995.

# 7

# What's New in Leading
# from the Edges?

Much creative leadership will come from the edges of organizations. A healthy look at where change comes from could even suggest that what some people perceive as 'the edges' of organizations are, in terms of creativity, their centres. In organizations like churches, which are designed to be 'flat', this is inevitable. Because there is a fundamental belief in equality or because they have a very small number of senior posts creative people will be close to the ground in most denominations. Even where a leader's influence becomes extensive their personal work may only be experienced in a local area and they may actually be known by a relatively small number of people.

Where to locate the centre and where the edge is an intriguing question. I have certainly heard some senior leaders say that they can be effective leaders only because they function at the edge of the organizations they lead. There are other leaders who never achieve seniority in their denomination who will be well known through their preaching, teaching, community activity or writing. Their influence will be far greater than the position they hold in a church or denomination. Neither of these types of leader will come into categories concerned with the practicalities of turning an organization around or developing a team of people in order to carry out operational tasks.

Leading from the edges puts us in good company. Jesus himself can only be described as such a leader. He had no place in the hierarchy of his faith and gained his reputation entirely by his personality, teaching, ideas and example. He did listen, value the outsider, challenge authority and build up a team of men and women who could share his vision and spread his teachings. In Chapter 5 we have already seen how Jesus drew together a group of disciples and followers and trained and motivated them. There are several models of leadership mirrored in his earthly ministry. We know from the biblical accounts of his last days that he experienced misunderstanding, mistrust, betrayal and desertion by his friends and supporters. All of these happenings and the feelings which go with them are experienced by everyone who undertakes the responsibilities of leadership, particularly those whose contribution is not recognized and who remain 'on the edges' for all of their work.

## From management to leadership

Before I move to heady examples of ways in which leadership comes from creativity at the edge I want to describe the place where significant leadership is exercised. This is through effective management and is seen where most people in the churches' work – at the local level in a parish or with a group of congregations. A Gallup research poll in 1998 interviewed 1,000 people who had recently left their jobs. Seventy per cent said that they had not left because of the job – they had left because the management was bad. Other British Medical Association research shows that working for a manager who is ineffective in some way can increase the risk of coronary heart disease by one sixth and the risk of a stroke by one third. In a Christian Research booklet, Jill Garrett, Director of leadership development at Caret, says 'The person who makes the biggest difference to culture and the emotional health of workers is the supervisor or manager who has the most contact with them'.[1]

Managers are leaders. They are the key people who bring about local change in a company or a department. For congregations much of the creative work which changes the local face of church life is brought about by an imaginative team rector or group ministry leader, rural or area dean, a circuit superintendent, regional minister or equivalent. It is precisely here, far from the heady heights of preferment, that a good mix of creativity and vision with managerial or organizational skills will bring about significant change.

In a piece of research commissioned by the DTI interviewing 5,000 people in their workplace they were asked 'What would inspire you to follow someone?' Answers which came back were concerned with the quality of management which puts inspiring leadership into practice. Incidentally, of the 5,000 people interviewed, one third said that they had never worked for an inspirational leader! (The DTI has a leadership guide which it has developed with Caret: www.inspiredleadership.org.uk. Log in and give yourself a self-knowledge leadership refresher.)

The qualities identified as allowing change to be brought about by good local management were these:

- *The ability to manage and engage people* Inspiration comes from a leader who listens, trusts, appreciates, has fun, shows they care and who involves everyone in what needs to be done.
- *Their personal make-up* Words such as 'determined', 'courageous', 'humble', 'patient' and 'vulnerable' were used. Words which do not sit easily together but which are there in the unusual but essential mix which creates the manager who is passionate, non-jargony, honest, reflective, respectful, committed and focused.
- *Their novel outlook* The local manager can have a flexibility which the senior leader, always in the spotlight, cannot have. Team leaders of this kind are valued because they think laterally, bend the rules, respond well to pressure, are highly accessible, have a vision about how their local piece of work can be developed and who are passionate about those they are there to serve.[2]

I am well aware that there is a resistance to the word 'manager' and the concept of managerialism in some church circles. It is quite easy to understand why this should be. Many people have had a bad experience of being managed, while others have certainly found that too much managerial reorganization has not necessarily improved their work situation. However, there are many important lessons to learn from good management and most of these apply themselves well to church situations. *They can look quite different and be inspiring when described as leadership from the edges.* More experiment and innovation is possible here than anywhere else. Good support for staff of the kind which gives them clear objectives and then allows them to be creative and get on with their tasks is deeply pastoral. There are particular ways in which managers are creative and by which they bring about lasting change.

1 *Managers embody hope.* This is my principal facet of good leadership; that it has this 'resurrection' new life element in it. The responsible manager will rally people around what they are doing and invite them to explore the many solutions there might be to a problem. This type of local leadership is essential for us in the churches. We do not know what shape they will take for the future. This can only be worked out by prayerful waiting on God and by creative local experiment. Denominational leaders cannot enthuse and deliver in this way. The local 'manager' can – and does. Here in these local groupings of congregations are, in my view, the workshops which are creating the shapes of our churches for the future.

2 *Managers enthuse and engage.* Those with designated local responsibilities are in the best place to be able to consult and then to draw in old and new faces who are energized by both the vision and the methods by which it is being turned into reality.

3 *Managers 'do' something.* The key task of the local leader is to turn ideas into action. Church leaders can have ideas and make pronouncements, synods and councils can pass policy resolutions but it is the local convener on the ground who has to turn these good ideas into practical realities. Here creativity and pragmatic common sense come together to give the kind of experimental action which will lead to practical solutions.

4 *Managers live their values.* The ways in which things are done, change is negotiated, difference reconciled and experiment reviewed reflect the values and beliefs which the manager has.

They also model the kind of culture and organization that the inspirational local person wants to create.

Here, in these descriptions of how change is brought about through local management, we can see leadership of another kind being exercised. This is not the high-profile work which attracts public attention and which may well set the overall direction of an organization. Such leadership is often more reactive to local conditions than we would want to acknowledge. This is change which is led through local hard work and determination. It is leadership which is trusted and valued but which gets as much blame and criticism as it does reward. That is because the local person or team on the ground has real opportunity to change things and make a difference. For some years it has interested me that the Church of England's National Deaneries Conference is always fully booked months before the event. That is because to this denomination the deanery, with its local lay and clerical leadership, has become a real workshop for change. Those engaged in this exciting but demanding work need places where they can get colleague support and where creative ideas and experiences can be exchanged.

## Creativity and marginalization

Most of those who are known as national or international leaders today have begun by doing a creative piece of work 'at the edges or on the margins' of their occupation. People like Bill Gates or the creators of many later internet facilities began in small, alternative or experimental situations. There are others who may be of more interest to us who have wanted to change society because they were affronted by the injustices which they saw around them. Some made their inspired contribution and died or remained in prison without seeing what they hoped for come about. The letters of Pastor Dietrich Bonhoeffer written from his prison cell testify to the amazing influence one modern theologian and thinker has had on subsequent generations. Others have lived and influenced from a marginalized position but have come to prominence through a change in political or economic circumstances. Tim Harle illustrated these situations with telling examples.

> In recent and contemporary politics, we can think of how, for many years, certain authority in South Africa emanated from a prison cell on Robben Island. Or how a significant source of authority in present day Myanmar comes from a suburban house in Rangoon.[3]

Such examples of situations we all know about are inspiring. They contrast with a certain sense of powerlessness or demoralization which seems to affect those in the midst of change. Harle points to a reflection by two other writers, Hamel and Prahalad, which connects with some feelings of powerlessness or demoralization expressed by local leaders and organizers in a denomination, and also by congregation members themselves.

> Front line employees and middle managers today, inclined to regard themselves as victims, have lost confidence in their ability to shape the future of their organizations. They have forgotten that historically it has been the dispossessed – from Gandhi to Mandela, from the American patriots to the Polish shipbuilders – who have led revolutions. Notwithstanding all the somber incantations that 'change must start at the top' one must ask how often the monarch has led a revolution.[4]

That is perhaps an easy or charged comment with which to end a quotation but it does contain the important reminder not only about where change begins but also that others have to lose position or give up/away power. When new energy is generated from a source which at first is experienced as at best an irritation but which develops into a movement with a momentum of its own, power and leadership shifts from one place to another. Georgeanne Lamont, among the most inspiring of modern business consultants and writers, points to the importance of change led not from the centre but from the margins of an organization.

She says that when a manager or leader is too 'snug' in the middle of a company – or a church structure – possessing power and comfort, they cannot always see what change is needed. It is often those on the margins who first experience changing conditions and the necessity for a new response.[5]

## CHARACTERISTICS OF LEADERSHIP FROM THE EDGES

The most important message about leadership from the edges is that this is the place where ideas and people come together in the most creative ways. There are three ways in which this different or alternative kind of leadership makes a particular gift to our wide understandings of how leadership supports and develops all that we do; it holds up a mirror to our activities and leadership styles, it leads from the future by imagining quite different futures and it listens generously to the marginalized and those who experience leadership from quite a different place.

Like Our Lord, many of those who have drawn followers around them have not intended to set up a new church or organization. When Roger Schutz set up his small, international, ecumenical community at Taizé he was developing a personal idea and calling as part of his own journey. What emerged is more significant, especially in the spiritual journey of young people, than could ever have been imagined. Mother Theresa's total identification with the poor and the objectives of the religious order she founded might have remained the province of a few had not the journalist and television personality Malcolm Muggeridge searched her out and featured her in a series of programmes. A little earlier, the work of George MacLeod in Glasgow and then with the foundation of the Iona Community, had a similar impact well beyond the dreams of its founder.

The newness and importance for us in the churches of this kind of leadership is the realization that change can come as much, or even more, from the edges of our organization as it does from its centre. The importance of leadership from the edges and the presence of the small alternative or pressure group organizations which live there is that they hold up a mirror to our churches as they are now. They ask direct and sometimes symbolic questions: Are you sure yours is the best way? Are there other ways to approach this? Can we work together on some alternative solutions? And, most importantly, are you sure you are listening to the people you are privileged to lead? The very existence of alternative organizations – or experimental ways of being church – challenges some of those in present positions of authority.

## It holds up a mirror

Really significant leadership from the edges can sometimes show up the inappropriateness or emptiness of policies and tried and tested ways when they have to address new situations. Leadership from the edges holds up a mirror to current leadership. Sometimes consultancy groups and training organizations as well as the research of academics show leadership themselves by holding up just such a mirror.

Sister Donna J. Markham, writing in the Jesuit magazine *Human Development*, sets out a humorous, if scathing analysis of the hollowness of some kinds of leadership when exposed to critiques by an outside group. She describes three caricatures of leadership found wanting when viewed by creative leaders from the edges.[6] She develops the idea that there are at least three types of leader today who are dangerous. They do not just keep a group or organization trapped in the present, they actually inflict harm because they hold out certainties and solutions that are no longer workable. The church or organization becomes 'sick' because it is trying to respond to the disturbed dynamics of its leadership. Informed caricature is one way to challenge leadership from a place on the edge.

- *The narcissist* Narcissists are found in leadership positions because their projection of power and drama and their uncanny knack for establishing quick, superficial relationships magnetize others into following them. The leader's promises cannot be fulfilled because personal fame and notoriety are more important to him or her than team building and commitment to the hard task of long-range vision. Consequently, any situation which challenges the Narcissist intensifies his or her feelings of powerlessness, and the Narcissist responds with vengeance, rage, and a backlash of autocratic control. When confronted, this leader frequently terminates his or her own position.

- *The empty suit* Suffering from a condition sometimes referred to as the 'Oz factor', the Empty Suit is intrinsically unable to lead from a sense of inner authority, so he or she must copy. The Empty Suit is a hollow person whose sense of leadership is devised from a superficial enactment of a role. To followers, the Empty Suit is someone who really seems to understand their every need and promises to take care of them, but nothing happens. Empty Suits have learned how to act and behave, but the inner substance is missing. The helping professions and social institutions such as the church and religious congregations have their share of these pseudo-leaders. They are deeply threatened by shared leadership . . . they waffle and procrastinate in decision-making. Consequently, the organizations they lead tend to become paralyzed. The advantage that Empty Suits have over Narcissists is that their level of subjective discomfort frequently leads them to seek professional consultancy.

- *The Talking Head* He or she is impervious to the feelings of others, lacks personal connection, and has little insight into how his or her overtly rationalized behavior affects others. Because Talking Heads negate or deny emotions, they are unable to function in team situations. Usually, these leaders experience some overwhelming organizational conflict they are unable to understand; this motivates them to seek consultation.

Such professional distance, used in skilled ways by consultants and therapists, by definition separated from the person or organization they are dealing with, give much more than just a mirror reflection of inappropriate leadership. They use detached skills to work with organizations and their leaders to analyse situations and develop ways forward. These 'new ways' will have had an initial life at the edges or on the margins of an organization before they are adopted by mainstream leaders or managers.

These caricatures offered by Markham have at their fundamental base a lack of spiritual depth which gives purpose and meaning to their life. The importance of value-based leadership for today's organizations has been established by Christians in business and by religious orders and lay communities offering a place where pressured leaders can explore again the original motivation for their work. Value-based and highly motivated leadership from the edges can speak to those in authority now. It can model and demonstrate key concepts of leadership, and show that they can be seen from another perspective. Energized leadership from the edges with the values given by faith communities can remind those who have lost their original vision or who are just 'burned out' that there are ways of walking with the Spirit and of rekindling new life.

Leaders for the church of the future need to be nurtured now in these values and to be confident in how to share them. Their tasks will be both to model their leadership values in the way they carry out their own tasks and roles and also to be 'beacons' of alternative leadership styles for those who continue working with models and methods they know no longer quite fit themselves or the work they have to do. Markham ends her article with a 'from the edges' challenge for leadership development in the churches.

> The church's leaders for the future must be excellent leaders, committed to building covenantal relationships through which the vision will be realized. They are mentors who are no strangers to suffering, who from the depths of their own belief express compassion and deep love . . . They are people who work deliberately and directly at establishing networks of teams that liberate the collective spirit of the group and place that power at the service of the community. They are risk takers who lead to places where some of us may be on our own.[7]

## It leads from the future

The 'Merlin Factor' is not a new idea in leadership teaching but it is new to our thinking about the place of leadership from the edges. It has been developed from reflective studies of how some companies have transformed themselves – *against all predictions and expectations*. The basis of the idea is, in theological terms, prophetic because it depends more on a vision of the future than on analyses of the present. The classic description of the Merlin Factor is simply stated: *what you choose for your future is more important than what you know about your past or present capabilities. It gives a vision of the future which cannot be predicted by present analyses.* Its title comes from the legendary Court of King Arthur and the Magician Merlin. Apparently there was a situation when Merlin had set breakfast for two people when no one could have known that they were expected. His answer was unusual in the extreme: 'I was born at the wrong end of time, and I have to live backwards from in front, while surrounded by a lot of people living forward from behind.'

That is an imaginative and creative way of describing what leading from the edges involves. Those who are setting up congregations without traditional understandings of clerical leadership are leading from the edge; those who are grouping congregations together and describing tomorrow's understandings of episcopacy are leading from the edge. Those who are building new congregations in house churches are pushing out the boundaries and disturbing traditional structures. Hierarchical church leadership, like monarchs in Hamel and Prahalad's example, are not going to innovate with this kind of reinterpretive leadership. But they do need to listen and to be able to work out how their denominations are already being changed by these new forms.

Merlin-like leaders, often beginning life on the edges of their organizations, start with a personal vision of their organization's future which is not necessarily based on assumptions about how it could adapt from the way it is now. Those who get promoted into the higher reaches of their denomination run the risk of forgetting or losing their original energy for change. The complexities and difficulties of the present are more than enough. They either become completely disconnected or renew themselves by still being willing to listen to and affirm those who are living creatively on the edges in the generations behind them.

The alternative for present leaders is to deny that these kinds of solutions and predictions have any kind of reality or place in their thinking. Davis Mills, editor of *The Evangelical Catholic* and director of publishing at Trinity Episcopal Church, Pittsburgh suggests that present and traditionally motivated leaders and their teams have five ways of responding to future-oriented leadership. They react by denial, centralization, homogenization, frantic activity or by cleansing. We might reflect that 'cleansing' has become one of the most favoured ways of deepening divisions in our churches again today. I have explored the reality of these divisions for a 'new-shape' church in Chapter 6. It is likely that the divisions and challenges described by Mills which bring those five reactions will not alone be resolved by dialogue with those who are energized and challenged by current conflicts. However, this dialogue has to go on, and to be led by the very best minds of those who are in the present leadership of our churches. Alongside this work of reconciliation and understanding will go new pieces of work which will be led from outside the structures. It will often be stimulated by the challenges of the secular world and by the rising profiles of other faiths.

The 'ceiling' on any attempt to change the strategic direction of an organization is the personal limitation of its executives. In this case these are our denominational leaders and senior lay members of their synods and councils. At the moment, whatever the leadership regards as possible becomes possible. Whatever alternatives they do not or cannot listen to become impossible. The first element in working with the Merlin Factor is to be able to 'think the unthinkable'. Tom Peters in *Thriving on Chaos* says, 'the chief job of the leader, at all levels, is to oversee the dismantling of dysfunctional old truths and to prepare people and organisations to deal with . . . change as innovations are proposed, tested, rejected, modified and adopted'. Those who are leading from the edges will be the people who bring the partially tried out ideas and those which work at their level, to be tried out on the larger stage.

The leader who has grasped the possibilities of thinking in the Merlin Factor ways will not be a stargazing futurologist or an undiscriminating adopter of the latest idea or fashion. They will be exercising a very refined kind of discernment, born of the values they hold and the resurrection leadership they embody. The reflective processes which the experienced, but still change-oriented, leader brings take an organization on to new places with unexpected pieces of analysis. 'Observe what everyone has observed but think what no-one else has thought' sums up for me this contribution of visionary leadership. Most people think about what they actually see, or have seen before, in order to determine that they think might be possible. The hoped-for spark of genius in the leader who can bring at-the-edges thinking into the centre is to look for, and discover, what is missing and to search for it in alternative solutions.

Many of the ideas for this reflection on leading from the edges using the Merlin Factor have come from an article by Charles E. Smith in the *Harvard Business Review* and were first published in 1990, though there have been many refinements since. I was most energized by one phrase in the middle of a quite dense text. It has a sense of the other about it which is, to the trained ear or sensitive soul, deeply spiritual:

All the executives interviewed for this article *listened generously in the present for the sound of the future.*

## It listens generously

To listen generously means to accept the need to explore how leadership from the edges can influence and change the thinking and nature of our organizations and of our churches. The Joseph Rowntree Foundation has published an important piece of action research by Mandy Wilson and Peter Wilde. It describes what processes can be used to 'listen generously', in their case to socially excluded communities. In our church life it can mean bringing into active commitment those who feel disaffected because their leaders do not appear able to listen to or value their contribution.[8]

They suggest 'benchmarks' which all those involved in a learning, listening and change programme might find valuable. They are the gifts brought by leadership from the edges:

- *Influence* Change is a subtle thing which energizes the work of local communities at the edges of society and shapes overall thinking in a range of ways. How the different parts of an organization speak to one another is capable of measurement and development.
- *Inclusivity* The ways in which large and well-established organizations consult their regions, branches and members are capable of analysis. The most frequent complaint of local people and of congregations is that they were not consulted or did not know that they were being consulted.
- *Communication* The processes by which information is shared and the procedures used are able to be monitored. Informal methods of communication are as important as formal ones and create different versions of reality. The communication structures and routes in an organization can value those at different places in the same ways.
- *Capacity* How resources are provided which allow communities and congregations to participate in the wider life of the whole can be analysed and described. Knowledge and skills can be shared between partner agencies and different congregations. The greater the availability of resources to local groups the greater will be their capacity to experiment with new forms and patterns of community.

The greatest groups who are 'on the edge' or outside the churches at the present are young people and young adults. Listening in a generous and careful way to their spiritual and religious needs is absolutely essential. The ways in which they will respond with their on-the-edges commitment is already very different. The acid test of whether or not leaders can listen deeply and generously and then guide change will be seen in how churches for the next generation can be open and inclusive to their ideas and to their needs.

This is a challenge from the edge not only from young adults to the Christian churches; it is a challenge from all young adults of faith groups to their religious leaders. Bilal Patel, who stood as an Independent candidate in the 2001 General Election, asserts that young British Muslims are disaffected because they believe that their elders 'kowtow' to politicians who refuse to give them an equal stake in British society.

> Many of us are annoyed with the older generations. The sort of leadership we need is something more radical than we have. But if you speak out as a young Muslim you are labelled as an extremist.[9]

## GROUPS WHICH LEAD FROM THE EDGES

I hesitate to enter this territory with too much enthusiasm because it is the ground I have occupied with many colleagues through the years of my own ministry. I will exercise the discipline of not describing those pieces of work which have been carried out primarily with the Edward King Institute for Ministry Development and with MODEM or the Industrial Christian Fellowship. It is my belief that as much change has been brought about by voluntary groups acting as 'critical friends' to the churches as has been achieved from initiatives which have begun in synods or by meetings of church leaders. Our modern church history in England is full of examples of such influence. From the Life and Liberty movement begun in the vicarage of St Martin-in-the-Fields in 1917 which set out to bring reform and more local participation in the Church of England (PCCs!) to the enormous growth and influence of the Alpha Courses which grew from the church of Holy Trinity, Brompton there are striking examples of change which began with leadership from the edges. My choice of one example allows us to see how a 'ginger group' began a change in thinking which influenced all the denominations and had an influence for good on the life of the people of Britain.

Christian Action was founded by a group of clergy and laity who wanted to see a much more assertive approach from Christian people and organizations in social and political reconciliation in the life of the nation and far beyond. It was founded from the Oriel fellowship in Oxford in 1946. The founder and first director was Canon John Collins, for more than 30 years a Residentiary Canon of St Paul's Cathedral, and well known for his involvement with the Campaign for Nuclear Disarmament. The story of Christian Action and its influence and achievements could be a book on its own. From 1979 to the late 1990s the organization was led by Canon Eric James. It was through the pressure group led by James and colleagues that Archbishop Robert Runcie was persuaded to establish a commission, chaired by Sir Richard O'Brien, 'To examine the strengths, insights, problems and needs of the Church's life and mission in Urban Priority Areas'. The consequent report *Faith in the City* aroused the conscience of the nation and led to the establishment of the Church Urban Fund, which initially raised £18 million for community projects in inner-city areas of England.

Just one very brief thumbnail account of the influence and achievements of a very well-known piece of leadership from the edges by pressure groups and organizations tells much, not only about what can be achieved, but also indicates the subtlety and complexity of leadership within our churches. We might rail against hierarchies and the still less than transparent methods of making senior appointments. The evidence is that as much leadership and direction setting comes from leaders who are at different places in the denominations, or outside them, as from within our church structures. The Spirit which God gives to believers and communities and the organizations which they form 'blows where it wills'. It often comes from far away places to give a refreshing sense of newness and re-formation.

## The centre and the edge

The debate about where real leadership which brings change comes from will go on for ever. Does it originate from the edge and influence the overall direction? We know and have described how this can happen. Can change come from the centre and through strategic centralized leadership? We also know that this can and does happen. That kind of leadership is most appropriate when major decisions of principle and policy have to be made. There is certainly a relationship between experiment and alternative ways and gradual changes of direction. The alternative view that the edges of an organization – in our case the parishes and local congregations of our churches – are the centre is attractive and probably more true that many would think. That the leadership is at the edge is often felt by those who are there. This kind of edge should not be an isolated and out-of-touch place. It can be the place where experiment and change are valued, where new ideas are placed alongside tradition and core beliefs and measured and, when the time is right, permission is given for the alternative journey of a few to become the highway to the future for many.

On just a few magical occasions, change is not gradual and an idea meets its time and comes of age. Leadership and management are done differently from then on. Things change and we want to live in a different way because we have seen a new part of God's truth and responded to a call to create a future different from what we and our colleagues had imagined. How that need for change can be recognized, led and consolidated is the subject of our next chapter.

### Notes

1. Jill Garrett, *Being Strategic about Leadership: The Principles that Work in God's World*, Christian Research Leadership Lecture, 2006, p. 6.
2. Garrett, *Being Strategic*, pp. 6–7.

3. Tim Harle, *Gimme 5! Multidisciplinary Perspectives on Leadership*. Published Papers of the International Colloquium, St George's House, Windsor, 5–6 September 2005, p. 19.
4. Gary Hamel and C. K. Prahalad, *Competing for the Future*, Harvard Business School Press, 1966, pp. xiif.
5. Georgeanne Lamont, *The Spirited Business: Success Stories of Soul Friendly Companies*, Hodder and Stoughton, 2002.
6. Donna J. Markham OP, 'Leadership for the Church's Future', *Human Development*, The Jesuit Educational Centre for Human Development, Spring 1994, Vol 15, No 1.
7. Markham, *Leadership*, p. 9.
8. Mandy Wilson and Pete Wilde, *Benchmarking Community Participation*, Joseph Rowntree Foundation, 2003.
9. *Disaffection among British Muslim Youth*, BBC News Online, 31 March 2004.

# 8

# What's New in Leading Change?

It is one thing to dream about change, or even to burn with frustration that the changes you want are not taking place. It is quite another thing to be able to analyse and understand a situation and then act in such a way that real and lasting change can be accomplished. In addition to understanding how structures enable or prevent change it is important to understand the feelings and reactions of those who are affected by changes. Change management is not new in many places. Managing change in such a complex organization as a denomination, or even a local congregation, requires sensitivity and inner resources which would test someone who has taken on less sophisticated organizations and won.

I have been influenced by the reflections of Penny Edgell Becker who wrote about conflict in congregations in six different denominations in the USA.[1] What is important in her work for our exploration of change is that she picked up a phrase about what she observed as a newcomer or observer to each of the congregations she visited. It was 'the way we do things here'. This piece of streetwise common-sense helped me to connect with writings and drawings which other consultants and observers have sent me and the brief phrase says much about the need to know the story and understand the culture of a congregation or denomination before change can be planned, agreed and implemented. I have put together the collective wisdom of many colleagues to form this chapter, and have added some experience of my own.

## What's new in resistance to change?

One way of understanding the implementation of change is to try and understand what is going on above and below the surface in the place where you are working. Knowing how and why they do things this way here is significant and important. A new leader will either enter a place where there is a long history of events and people or be promoted from within with hopes and reactions coloured by a particular view of the church or denomination.

Sir John Harvey-Jones, in his book *Making It Happen*, writes with wisdom and experience about how it feels to take on the top job:

> After all, for many years you have watched the mistakes and blunders of your predecessors. You have always been aware of the things that have gone wrong, and have always believed that more could be done, or that things could have been done in different ways, or more effectively . . . you have already formed a number of ideas about what you would like to do, almost invariably in terms of correcting what you see as being the mistakes of the past. You are conscious that you need to 'grasp' the organisation immediately. You must move quickly if you are to convey the image of determination and clarity that you will need if you are to establish your leadership and achieve your ends. Furthermore, the responsibility lands on you suddenly, almost without warning. Neither you, nor your colleagues, or your company are likely to take kindly to you spending your first three months in a secluded location, doing what you really ought to do, namely thinking.[2]

Some of the stories, myths and reactions you inherit will undoubtedly arise from the experiences, damage done and successes of the leaders who have produced the events and strategies which have shaped the immediate past. It is important to be seen to listen to the stories and to understand what is behind the way they are being told now. Even if you cannot go away to a secluded location to think you do need to spend much of the first three months listening.

## 'Hard' elements in resistance

An organization will have its own symbols and special or sacred places and these will have their own developed methods for resisting change. Parts of a building will 'belong' to a certain group. Statues or hymn books or kneelers or other furnishings will represent growth at a certain stage and cannot be changed without causing offence in some quarter. Events, meetings, celebrations and saints days can have strong symbolic meaning. The new leader rides roughshod over these at their peril.

Whoever has a certain title in an organization may not be the actual leader of that group or activity. Activities in long-standing organizations like congregations or denominations may well be the result of long periods of attrition reflecting the ways in which power struggles have been resolved. Figure 6 sets out these 'soft' elements of resistance to change in an easy and accessible way. They are accompanied by another group which contain 'hard' elements of resistance of a different kind.

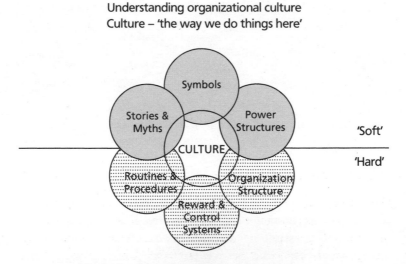

Figure 6: Problems in implementing strategic change

## Hard elements in resistance to change

'The way we do things here' can be demonstrated in no better a place than the routines and procedures which form the cement of week-by-week, year-by-year activity. Almost all clergy will say that they have to see a congregation through a full year before they get to know who has what job in which season.

Reward and control systems will have been used by your predecessor and are used by the group leaders you will inherit. You will use the method yourself to get some things done and to guarantee some agreements. In an organization like a church with very few sanctions the use of rewards and incentives are frequently the only way forward. Control systems are used by those who like the rule book and the small print of an organization. Sometimes resorting to legalism can be a way of defending your position as well as resisting change.

You will also have to work within the limits, doctrines and boundaries of your denomination. Ways of working are set from other places in your denomination. There is always a tension between being too comfortable in a denomination as it is and the frustration of wanting to kick over the traces and take unilateral action. Some people, leaders or not, leave a denomination if they think it is moving away from them – or they from it.

Leading change with these human and organizational constraints is subtle and very difficult indeed. There are many pieces of analysis which can go alongside wisdom and experience which will allow a leader or leadership team to develop strategies which will establish lasting change.

## Making sure change changes

To the experienced eye there are many recognizable features in the process of change. Many of these are human and touch on natural and perfectly normal feelings as any one of us or any group we are associated with is confronted with change. There are parallels with the processes associated with bereavement but these should not be pushed too far. More likely, the experienced leader will see sophisticated systems like those 'soft' and 'hard' ones described here which will come into play to prevent change. Most of those involved will not know how refined their methods of resistance have become.

Figure 7 sets out processes and patterns of behaviour associated with change. The shock of having to behave differently or come to terms with a new situation can be overwhelming. First reactions can range from feelings of inability to cope to numbness brought on by realization that the familiar and well-known will be taken away. This anxiety is followed either by a temporary retreat into the things which give security or to an attempt to seek allies and draw others into a conspiracy of resistance. It can also lead to a false confidence that the skills already exist to do whatever is being asked.

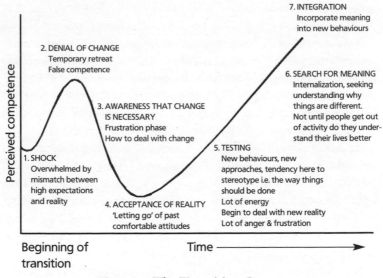

Figure 7: The Transition Curve

Once the shock and panic associated with a disturbing situation have passed there begins to dawn an awareness that things could not have gone on as they were before and that change is necessary.

Implementation is a heady time. New ways are tested out with varying degrees of success. Enormous energy is expounded; there is frustration and disappointment that not everyone is on board and putting in maximum energy. Those driving the change and those who have been won over to the need for change will experience frustration that plans and new activities and structures take so long to be negotiated and brought in. There is anger and frustration as different members of a team react each in their own way to whatever is going on. People are scapegoated if they resist or fail, others are caricatured if they even seem to resist by asking real questions about the wisdom of how some things are being done. As the new activities and structures link together in a visible way to the overall strategy a time to reflect needs to be built in. Here is the important time for a first piece of evaluation and review. What has worked? What needs adapting through use? What did not work and what has been learned from the experience?

Reflective practice, this time of objective review, allows new ways to become internalized. This is what our organization or church is like now and we have been a part of it. All the experiences and tensions of leadership have been travelled. The pain of seeing an inevitable path and not being supported by many who might have been trusted have become clear. The death of old ways is happening as new life and a different future begins to unfold. These are just the same reactions as those experienced by the first followers of Jesus. Then there was the problem of how to begin to build a network of slightly differing, personality led, churches. Now there is the challenge of gradual adaptation as an organization with a long history moves in this transitional way to the shapes God is calling it to have for the future.

Some of the elements of review arising from reflective practice can be seen in Figure 8.

The difficulties encountered will be many. It is not helpful to consign them to the past or to put them in a 'too difficult box' to be dealt with later. They need immediate initial evaluation with those involved. If this does not happen, strange pieces of behaviour emerge from colleagues or groups at unexpected times. They

|  | Programmes | Projects |
|---|---|---|
| Goals and objectives | High-level goals | Specific objectives of time, cost and performance |
| Definition | Not clearly defined | 'Frozen' and change controlled |
| Timescale | Open ended – longer | Fixed, shorter |
| Logical sequence | Not necessarily fixed | Fixed |

**Figure 8: Characteristics of programmes and projects**

| Factors viewed as either important or absolutely critical | |
|---|---|
| Communicating a clear vision | 100% |
| Staff participation | 100% |
| Instilling process ownership | 95% |
| Process improvement teams with staff from all levels | 90% |
| Instilling a change culture | 90% |
| Organizing staff around the process | 90% |

*Source:* University of Bristol Survey Report 'Business Process Re-engineering in the UK Financial Services Industry'

**Figure 9: Implementing organizational change:
the most important factors**

each need to tell someone, to make their point one more time or to heal themselves and address their fatigue by hitting out in some way.

The results of a survey from the University of Bristol (Figure 9) help to describe the importance of involving as many people as possible in each of the stages of change.

## PERSONALITY AND CONTEXT

I now want to examine what I believe to be the two least recognized factors in understanding how change can be brought about. The first is that people with different personalities will approach the challenge of bringing about change in different ways. There is not one model or example of individual or team leadership which will fit all situations. Knowing who you are when the responsibility for bringing about change is placed upon you is very important indeed. Such self-knowledge will help you to survive the stresses and strains of the challenge. It will also help you to understand that if you are to be effective you need to form a team made up of personality types complementary to your own.

The second factor, which I regard as enormously undervalued, is the need to understand that in bringing about change 'one size fits all' solutions are disastrous. I have seen very little writing about understanding the context in which change is brought about. Very few 'how to' or understandings of systems books really take into account the size of the denomination or congregation before they come up with grids, diagrams, models and solutions. It is particularly important to know that different approaches to bringing about change will be needed with small, middle-sized or large congregations. Teams and groups will need another approach. The small diocese or district will need leadership and devolved management in a different way than the large one covering an enormous and varied geographical area. Cathedrals are yet another story!

### Personality and skills

Leslie Francis and Mandy Robbins have written most intriguingly about how different personality types approach their place and roles in religious organizations and even why different people are attracted to work in different denominations.[3] They use their widely respected expertise to explain how different personality types as identified in the Myers-Briggs indicators explain attitudes to change and to particular approaches to ministerial and denominational work. They also explain how the revised Eysenck Personality Questionnaire, first published in 1985, identifies indices of extraversion, neuroticism and psychoticism with regard to personality.

They ask a very interesting question which I have not seen explored elsewhere: do different denominations attract into ministry people with significantly different personality profiles? They go on to explore the answers to this question with shrewd observations, all based on their research. What is it about some ministers that make them more able than others to grow and lead large congregations? Why do some ministers give more weight to preaching than others? Why do some like pastoral care and visiting? Why are some more at home in secular or community settings and why do some enjoy time spent with computers, developing bureaucracies and attending denominational committees? They ask why different personality profiles value different aspects of ministry. Most importantly, they go on to ask whether it would be strategically important to locate the right kind of minister in the local situation which required their particular skills. This question, and the demand for a positive and affirmative answer, is central to understandings of the types of person and team required to initiate and manage change at different levels in our churches.

## Personality and the leadership of change

Using the Eysenck Personality Scales published in 1991 Francis and Robbins help us to understand, as I interpret their descriptions, ways in which different personalities will approach the leadership and management of change.

The extravert personality is sociable, gregarious and develops a wide range of people to talk to. Change is addressed in the public forum. Everyone will know that new ideas are being explored. Many will tremble at the scale of what is being put forward, while others will be excited and want to associate themselves with what is happening. The extrovert leader will be in a hurry, want people around them in their team who are energized and also in a hurry and who might be willing to experiment and take chances. The whole team will be optimistic, relatively light-hearted and will give out a sense that things are on the move. The nature of such personalities and groups means that the pace needed and the energy engendered will make the work veer towards a 'command and control' style, not least because the pace expected is fast. The danger of such a method is that, while issues are addressed rapidly and short-term solutions are found, lasting creative change can be absent. This style has been criticized because it has the danger of being too fast moving and thus superficial, can fall into the trap of being able to 'fix but not innovate'.

The introvert leader and their team will be introspective, want much analysis done before any moves are made, will be perceived almost as 'secretive'. The change they bring about or plan will be regarded as understood by only a few with the danger that most people have the impression that 'they do not know what is going on'. The advantage of this approach is that plans are thoroughly researched and have a low risk factor. Change may be more gradual, but more lasting. It may come through a 'predict and prevent' approach rather than a high profile, 'find out and fix' one.

In terms of leadership the Eysenck scale also helps us to understand how what is called 'neuroticism' affects and influences change. This is important because feelings as well as actions are all wrapped up in approaches to change. These types of person or team will show higher emotional characteristics. The whole organization, congregation or district may develop the team's characteristic of anxiety and worrying. Public meetings may be tense and over-react to what is being proposed. Emotional judgements can give a disproportionate reaction to the need for change. Everything gets turned into a crisis which needs overwork and sleepless nights from the whole team to bring about a resolution.

The scale also looks at a most interesting area which I have heard described by many who have had a bad experience of an oppressive team or a dominant leader. This is the place where Eysenck describes those who score highly on the psychoticism scale. Here there can be a tendency to be cruel and inhumane. The pressing need for change can be used to excuse intolerable behaviour. There may be hostility, even to old friends, trusted colleagues and team members. There can be a disregard for danger and a perceived enjoyment in making fools of other people. Empathy, feelings of guilt and sensitivity to other people are notions which are strange and unfamiliar to such leaders and leadership groups.

Such descriptions as these are easily caricatured and can seem over analytical or simplistic. In exploring these types myself I have been able to associate my experiences with some of these characteristics and to understand why I have found some change situations and leadership groups difficult. Even this small lifting of a lid helps to demonstrate that change is a sophisticated and complex activity. The personality of a leader will influence the way change is brought about and the team which is brought in to support what is being planned and then executed.

What is thought to be 'good' or 'bad' may also depend on the culture of a denomination. It may also explain why some denominational leaders appear to be at worst dysfunctional or at best ill at ease with the leadership position they have. Francis and Robbins point to a number of studies which show that male Anglican clergy, Roman Catholic priests and Methodist ministers are significantly more introverted than men in general. The same studies show that much of the work which is expected to be done is work shaped for extroverts. Introverted ministers find high-profile public appearances and much contact with many people draining. Training, support and team balance is needed for the most effective use to be made of such people. Equally, those who make appointments, especially senior ones, need to be especially sensitive to the danger of appointing or over-promoting the smaller number of extroverts in a denomination.

Interestingly, the same studies show that in the free Evangelical and Pentecostal churches there is a much higher than average tendency to attract extrovert ministers or pastors. Such people tend to find it easier to attract more men into congregations and leadership teams than do introverts, who display more 'feminine' characteristics. The rise of evangelicalism in traditional denominations in recent years has also brought about a series of different approaches to change. Some of these changes fail because they are applied from a different, sometimes transatlantic context to congregations with a very different history and of a very different size who have less potential for change and development. It is this analysis of size which we now need to place alongside the serious need to understand personality when we are analysing or planning strategic change.

## SIZE AND CHANGE LEADERSHIP

All experienced ministers know that they have succeeded in some areas of their work in one place but have been less successful, or failed, in another while using much the same methods, with of course, their same personality. One factor in this is that they have been working with different sized congregations or in a different type of organization. The size of a congregation and its separatedness or its relationships with other local congregations can make all the difference. Here I want to develop and take further in an English context a formative piece of work done by the Alban Institute in the USA.[4]

### New leadership in the small congregation

Congregations of 20 or less tend to be static. Only a very few of these will have their own individual minister, though some will have exclusive 'use' of a part-time or unpaid minister. The particular characteristic of such small congregations is that they will not be used to welcoming and initiating newcomers. Those who form the congregation will have fought many battles together, and some against each other. They will live in a kind of tension born of defensiveness and the need to survive.

Such small congregations will have a long history which will be held and kept fresh in the memory by some members. It is a frequent experience that such small groups will be made up of a number of families with a few significant other people. There will be dominant characters which I have described in some of my other writings as patriarchs and matriarchs. Writing about such small local groups in the United States, Roy Oswald of the Alban Institute has said that ministers tend not to stay too long, with the consequence that they make little difference and what they change gets changed back when they leave.

There are various ways in which change can be brought about in such places. The main one is for consistent policy and care to be given over a long period of time. This will best be offered if ministerial support is given from a wider grouping and the minister whose chief responsibility this is has colleague support and stimulation elsewhere. The bringing together of small congregations, urban and rural, into loose groupings and federations allows for steady development. It also provides a wider range of places where young people and young adults can meet together, where baptism and confirmation/membership preparation can be given and where overall policy and direction can be debated.

Small congregations are places where the members find it less easy to travel to share life with other small or large congregations. Some members will never attend any other than their own church – they see it as a kind of disloyalty which will be 'punished' by closure. Others will gradually flourish and grow as they make new friends and begin to catch a wider vision. Newcomers can find it hard to join the small congregation. In one of my own surveys about size and growth one response by a newcomer was 'there is nowhere to hide in the small congregation'.

The type of sensitive leadership needed to nurture the small congregation is a specialism in itself. That this type of work is now being given serious consideration shows in one of our interesting statistics – that more growth is taking place in the small congregation than almost anywhere else. Perhaps it is also because here the seeker can find a human-sized community made up of people who, if well prepared, can give time and genuine support to them.

## New leadership in middle-sized congregations

Congregations of 60–120 are the most familiar type of grouping and, to many people and denominational leaders, look and feel like the ideal church. Such congregations are sometimes called family or pastoral sized. They have all the characteristics of busyness and some success. Because of their apparent self-sufficiency they can be among the hardest places to bring about change. Their strength is in their resilience. They can look successful and many are. They have to draw in ten or more new members each year to compensate for loss or death. Hardest of all to change are these congregations where there is a sizeable number who brought about an earlier renewal and who look back to a successful but fading past.

The congregation paying its bills and holding its own numerically may just still be able to be provided by the denomination with its own minister. Increasingly, this will not be the case as full-time ministers become fewer. One consequence is that new styles of leadership will need to be developed. Local ministry or leadership teams need to be established and sustained alongside the formal church council of whatever kind. A minister with two or three such congregations will need to develop extremely sophisticated skills of delegation and consultation. Congregations will need to be led on from the 'bereavement' and perceived loss of status which comes from not being able to continue to have their own full-time resident minister. Prominent members of such congregations are likely to be angry with their denomination. While paying more for membership or affiliation through some kind of common fund, less will be coming back in ministerial support and denominational resources. It is not surprising that there is more confusion and low morale in this size of congregation than in any other.

It is almost a new kind of church, or at least of ecclesiology (how we understand church) that is being developed here. In this situation leadership, while not being thanked and applauded, is pioneering new ways. Teamwork is of the essence. Ministers grouped together to cover a large area will need to be chosen in ways which meet local needs and which bring in specialisms. Local churches will be organized and administered either by a local group or by a paid, central lay administrator. Experience is growing in these areas and new networks are being formed.

Initial and inservice training has yet fully to come to terms with this new situation. It also seems appropriate to say that the initial call to ministry needs to be developed or re-educated so that a call to ministry and priesthood in these new situations can appear attractive in new ways. The new patterns of leadership, and team leadership, which are emerging from these new situations have yet to be evaluated and appraised. Such work is now overdue. It is one of my fears that both potential clergy and committed laity will not respond to their calling if the work appears too stressful and those engaged in it are either exhausted or on the edge of despair.

## New leadership in the large congregation

Here there are considerable leadership and redirection issues which have to be faced in a very public arena. There seems to be widespread concern that membership and numbers in large congregations, of 150 or more, are not holding up. Some places are highly specialized and act as a 'transit camp' for those coming new to the faith. Others have had a day of greatness centred around a charismatic minister or major musical or cultural activity and the prime movers have gone. Other large congregations have been eclectic, with civic or community responsibilities and have drawn in a kind of churchgoer that is gradually ceasing to exist.

Life is very difficult for present or new ministers in such places. They have high expectations placed on them and are perhaps expecting much of themselves. They struggle with the tension between keeping up a large church with a past which is still a close and strong memory and leading a congregation on to the new roles which a building of this kind can fulfil in what is often a very changed town or city. My observation is that leadership in the 'large' congregation is reinventing itself. There seems to be a realization that whatever gave identity and purpose for a previous generation cannot be revived. Such active places are designing new roles for themselves. Many have established interesting cultural activities and restaurants in other buildings for which they have responsibility. Some run, and profit from, enormous community activities while others gain funds and staff through chaplaincies to the technology parks and industries which characterize flourishing towns and cities. Few continue to exist without some major partnership or shared, income-generating uses for their buildings. I am aware that this situation is completely different from that in the USA where 'large' churches have a membership counted in thousands.

Such innovative diversity requires much from leaders and leadership teams. Some of these large congregations will flourish because they are centres of excellence for their particular ministry or churchmanship tradition. While affirming in some ways, such speciality puts that congregation and its ministers in a competitive relationship with their neighbouring churches and congregations. For such churches to flourish and develop there needs to be clear affirmation and strategic support from the leadership of a denomination. Such congregations will be likely to pay more into their denomination than they get from it and will feel that they are supporting smaller brother and sister congregations. The challenge from particularly specialized places with their ministers is how to lead their people and order their lives in such a way that they remain fully committed to the life of their denomination. Such a challenge needs to be reciprocal. Church leaders and denominational committees need to value the significant and high-profile work done by such churches and to thank and affirm them accordingly.

## New leadership challenges in cathedrals

In England, and in my experience also across mainland Europe, cathedrals are among the most interesting places showing church growth. While large-congregation churches are, in the main, struggling to keep their profile, cathedrals attract increasingly

large numbers both to their regular services and to ones designed
for special occasions. I am not aware of any detailed research into
how and why cathedral numbers are growing and consequently
evidence has to be anecdotal.

It is clear that many regular churchgoers who become dis-
enchanted with their local parish church move towards cathedrals. Others who prefer an ordered liturgy with a high standard
of choral music also gravitate to these places. It is also the case
that many who like to worship in relative anonymity without
wanting to be drawn into the increasingly 'family' or 'membership' stances of local congregations find what they want in the
large building with its many services and congregations which
come and go with relative freedom. The cathedral atmosphere
also conveys a sense of the numinous and of mystery, which adds
considerably to the sense of the presence of God in hallowed and
ancient places.

For staff who come new to cathedrals there is frequently a
sobering sense of shock. Most will have come into cathedral life
through a significant piece of work elsewhere and will have
attracted the notice of those in the preferments system. More and
more will have come to cathedral staff membership through a
process of open advertising. The first shock for many who have
'run their own show' before – perhaps a large parish church – is
that they are members of a team and have to work with colleagues
while not themselves being the team leader. For those who have
come to canonries many will have a developed specialism of pastoral care, liturgy or music. Yet others will only be part-time at
their cathedral and will have the divided loyalty of another piece
of work or responsibility within the diocese. The leadership roles
for each will have been changed in significant ways.

To be appointed a cathedral dean is to accept one of the greatest challenges the church can offer. These posts have failed more
than any others, especially in the Church of England, in recent
years. Reasons for the difficulties associated with becoming a
dean are many. At the heart of these lies the complex system
which is a cathedral. Some who come into the post have little or
no experience of managing a multi-million pound asset, housed

in a beacon heritage site, with a range of staff some of whom are paid and many more of whom are volunteers.

As I understand it, there are two general types of cathedral in England, though some of those in them do not like or accept the distinction. On the one hand, the parish-church cathedrals are of relatively recent origin and have been 'upgraded' from parish-church status when their diocese was created. The building is not over large and will have been extended at various stages in its life to allow its new status and functions. There is likely to be a regular congregation of not more than that of a good parish church, but with more duties and responsibilities and more staff to work alongside. However, members of the congregation do not have a PCC by which they can make their voice heard – and manage change. There are layers of government from Cathedral Council to Chapter and Fabric Advisory Committee, each made up of nominees from other places and who may not worship regularly at the cathedral or come at all to its principal events. Some of those who come to work here find the setting to be smaller in scale than their previous work, and the complexity of relationships perplexing and frustrating. There are networks of colleagues who give self-help but, as yet, there is no national structure on offer to support and develop staff appointed to such positions.

The historic cathedrals, on the other hand, have many of the same complexities but face challenges on a different scale. While there may be endowments, there are also maintenance costs which reach new heights year on year. Heritage grants are available as is the possibility to charge for entrance. Nevertheless, almost all such buildings teeter on the edge of financial viability, and will do so until new systems of national support are put in place. To become a dean in such a significant place as an ancient cathedral is no small challenge. To expect the man or woman appointed to grapple in an effective way with the leadership of this prestigious public place requires more support and training than is currently available. In addition to cathedral responsibilities, the dean will form part of the bishop's senior staff and have a wider leadership role in the diocese.

In spite of all these frustrations and complexities, or because of them, cathedrals flourish. More and more people seem to find in them the sense of purpose and the pointers to meaning in their lives for which they are searching. What are cathedrals doing which is right? This needs to be the question which should be explored. Their success may not continue unless the most appropriate support systems are put in place to enable effective team leadership to develop or be sustained.

## Leadership and change in new-shape local congregations

Here the newness and urgency for new solutions continues apace. The situation is complex. Much has emerged through significant and real changes:

- the growth of new groups encouraged by 'fresh expressions' initiatives;
- the development of the cell-church and house-church movement;
- the lowering of denominational allegiances;
- the need to create worshipping groups in hospitals, prisons, and the workplace and around the needs of different professions.

Bishop John Robinson experienced house churches and the Eucharists celebrated in the homes of worker priests in France in the 1950s. In his book *On Being the Church in the World* he has an essay called 'The house church or the parish church'. In a prophetic way he describes the theological interrelatedness of our variety of different contemporary Christian groupings very well. In this reflection I can see a church leader acting both as an encourager and influencer of change and a keeper and developer of our theological and ecclesiological tradition.

> The conception of the cellular structure of each parish, reflecting the cellular structure of each diocese, is something that has previously been lost in the modern Church. We should never think of a diocese as being an agglomeration of individuals or a federation of local organizations, but always an *organic* union of parishes.

The house church is essentially the same mixture as the lump, except the area of natural community is smaller and may, in these days when communities are not geographical at all, be outside the parish structure altogether.

The house church represents, so to speak, the tap roots of the vine, that of the life of the tree most closely in contact with the clinging soil of everyday existence.

The house church, if it is really the whole church in microcosm must reproduce the 'marks' of catholicity – the Apostles' teaching and fellowship, the breaking of bread, and the prayers.

I believe that the cellular structure of the Church will be rediscovered as a necessity of its life.[5]

To 'lead' such a confederation of units is somewhat of a misnomer. While the general public and very many people in the pews expect the senior person to act something like a managing director or chief executive of a medium-sized company, those struggling with these positions find the experience rather different. If leadership in these significant places is to be effective Robinson's analysis must be understood in new ways.

## Senior leaders and local experiment

What's new is the reinterpretation of role. The senior person is a facilitator, an influencer, a public representative figure and the guardian of the tradition from which their appointment has sprung. In what ways do they lead their organization? They will be the people with the greatest overview. They will have the episcopal or oversight role of understanding where their people are in the structures of their organization. What's new is that they will come to know that they cannot keep this knowledge and technical oversight to themselves. They will concentrate on building a leadership team who will be committed to many and diverse aspects of the life of a diocese, district or province and who will develop agreed plans to carry through to the next stages those strategies devised by synods and boards.

What's new is the realization that those in senior leadership in a denomination have more influence than power and that they will have learned to use it for the development of their leadership strategies. In his most recent book on the use of power Bishop Stephen Sykes has pointed out that there are particular responsibilities given to church leaders.[6] They do have patronage and can use the appointments which they make to reinforce what it is they and their staff team have decided to do. They also have the responsibility to use discipline when necessary. The newness is in working out how to be a public figure, alongside colleagues, increasingly of other faiths, while holding together pastoral and disciplinary responsibilities in a fragile and adapting system of local churches.

This will all be done in the diversity which is the modern life of faith. Church leaders and leadership teams will themselves be made up of people nurtured in one or other of the streams which make up church today. BUT as leaders they represent the WHOLE Church and have to learn the painful task of setting aside party allegiances and aspirations and put on themselves the catholicity and clothing which will enable them to become more and more the focus for unity of the whole people of God. Their representative place in the organization is to move it all forward with the teaching influence and executive levers which have been given to them.

New-shape leaders will look less and less like the leaders who were their inspiration and model. They will bring with them their experience and their knowledge. They will learn not to become shaped and limited by the present form of the organizations they serve but will lead change in their churches because they have been schooled in a faith which has at its heart both the cross and the resurrection. This can only mean that through the pain and suffering of desertion and death an ever new resurrection body will emerge. It is the leadership teams in our churches, both at the centre and on the edges, who have a vital part to play in making this resurrection possible. The shape and form of this body we have yet to discern. The search and the gradual process of revelation are what make these demanding tasks worthwhile. This faith is the source of our motivation and the fount of our energy.

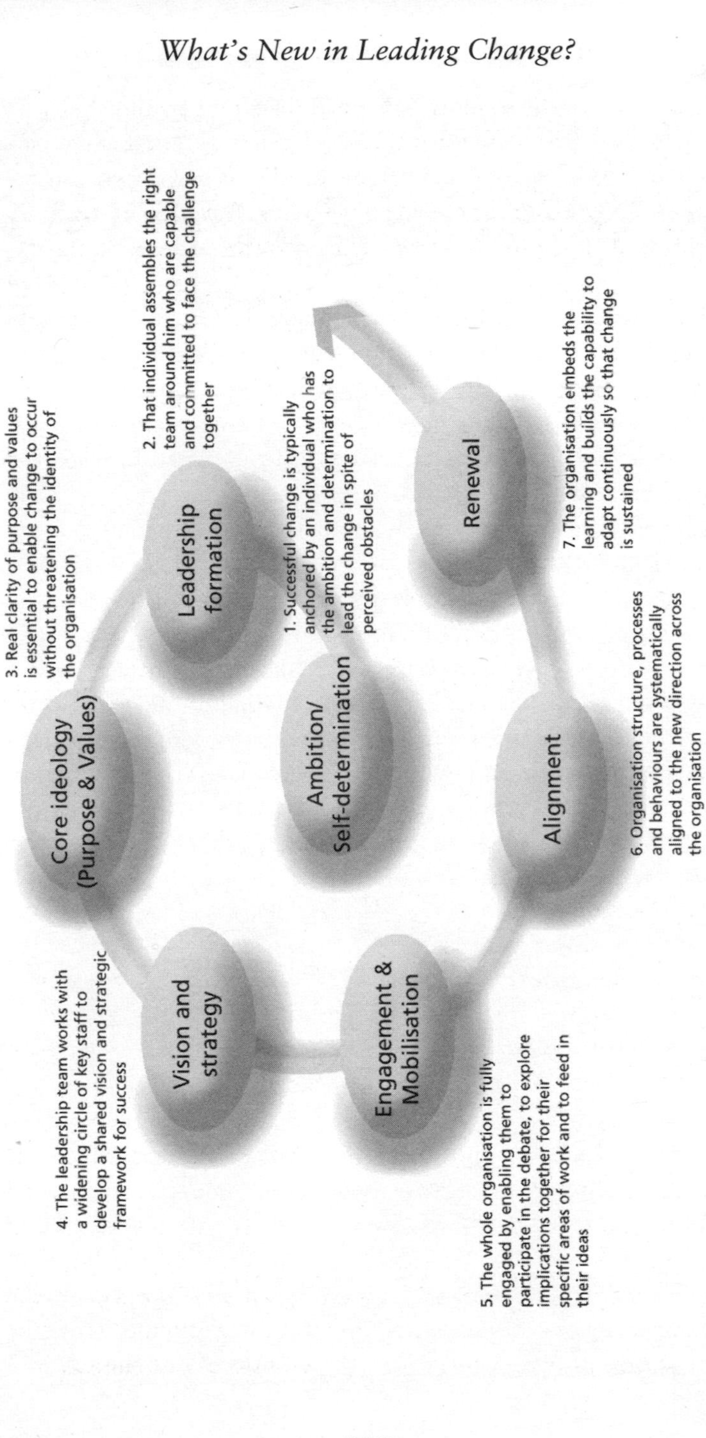

Figure 10: Sustaining success

**Leadership formation**

2. That individual assembles the right team around him who are capable and committed to face the challenge together

3. Real clarity of purpose and values is essential to enable change to occur without threatening the identity of the organisation

**Renewal**

7. The organisation embeds the learning and builds the capability to adapt continuously so that change is sustained

**Ambition/ Self-determination**

1. Successful change is typically anchored by an individual who has the ambition and determination to lead the change in spite of perceived obstacles

**Core ideology (Purpose & Values)**

**Alignment**

6. Organisation structure, processes and behaviours are systematically aligned to the new direction across the organisation

**Vision and strategy**

4. The leadership team works with a widening circle of key staff to develop a shared vision and strategic framework for success

**Engagement & Mobilisation**

5. The whole organisation is fully engaged by enabling them to participate in the debate, to explore implications together for their specific areas of work and to feed in their ideas

## REVIEW AND REFLECT

The diagram with which I bring this chapter to a conclusion (Figure 10) has very generously been made available for open use by the Telos Partnership. It reminds us that the situations within which we work are never static. The most significant way to remain aware of the changes taking place around us – and of the changes taking place within us – is through designing and structuring a constant process of personal and team review.

Review begins with the attention we give to ourselves. We need to remain fresh and to keep alive the sources of our own motivation. The right team gradually assembled produces its own rewards in terms of developing and leading change in any organization. The distinct sense of purpose which the team develops becomes infectious. It is only then that those with whom the senior team works can develop strategies with which others can identify and work to carry out. Consistent team leadership, carried out with character and integrity, will gradually infuse the organization, congregation, parish district or diocese with the values of leadership and work to which God continues to call and lead them. What comes next is the need to know how well you are doing and how to look after yourself in this exhilarating but energy-sapping exercise of leadership.

### Notes

1. Penny Edgell Becker, *Congregations in Conflict: Cultural Models of Local Religious Life*, Oxford University Press, 1999.
2. John Harvey-Jones, *Making it Happen: Reflections on Leadership*, Collins, 1988, pp. 184–5.
3. Leslie J. Francis and Mandy Robbins, *Personality and the Practice of Ministry*, Grove Booklets Pastoral Series P97, 2004.
4. See Malcolm Grundy, *Understanding Congregations*, Cassell Mowbray, 1998 and *What They Don't Teach You at Theological College*, Canterbury Press Norwich, 2003.
5. John A. T. Robinson, *On Being the Church in the World*, SCM Press, 1960, p. 85.
6. Stephen Sykes, *Power and Christian Theology*, Continuum, 2006.

# 9

# What's New in Consultancy and Review?

Perhaps it is just selfish but we do like to know how well we are doing. What other people think of us has to be a question nagging away deep down even for the outwardly self-assured. I still remember as an anxious teenager reading a piece of wisdom from that homespun advice magazine the *Reader's Digest*. It said something like 'however much you wonder what people are thinking of your performance remember that they are equally or more anxious about what you think about them'. At much the same time I read another piece of similar wisdom from a book about developing self-esteem. It said that everyone needs the equivalent of padding in their shoes to make them feel that they are walking just that little bit taller. Each of us develops ways of coping when things are difficult and even of rewriting really bad events so that they do not seem so grim or disastrous in retrospect.[1] That might suit some of the situations we are faced with in life. If we are being professional and responsible we now need to take into account the vast range of opportunities which help us with our own development and to know how we are doing in relation to what is expected or hoped of us.

More profoundly, such an exploration is about personal integrity. We all know that the work we do and the environment of that work puts pressure on us and influences our behaviour in subtle ways. A number of people I talk to in positions of heavy responsibility comment how much they worry that the job is taking them over. They talk about their concern that they are developing into a person who is not really their true self as a result of having to behave in certain ways in their job. This is no less true for clergy, indeed for some it is even more so. Many men and women feel pressured to behave in certain ways because of the expectations placed upon them. They worry that 'the collar' or the uniform gives them something to grow into or to hide behind. The public role of a clergyperson influences their behaviour, gives a certain sense of security and allows idiosyncrasies to be developed, not always for the best.

## Leadership review in our churches

An enormous change has taken place in the ways in which denominations see and use their clergy and in how they understand the life of their congregations. Within the overall context of Christianity as a missionary movement much of church life and ways of operating were seen as static. Clergy were placed in a parish to work with a congregation without too much thought about what they would do or what they would achieve. Congregations rose and fell in relatively small ways with the core of regulars holding things together in an adequate way, being energized by their particular cultural tradition. Clergy would service and support a congregation but would spend much more time in the life of their local community or in carrying out a particular activity which interested them. Many clergy in the seventeenth and eighteenth centuries were academics, scholars, researchers, and scientists. Few people, and certainly not their bishop, took an interest in what they were doing, or in what they might be expected to do.

These characteristics of clerical and congregational life have now changed. Jobs are analysed and described with some accuracy. The scarce and expensive resource of clergy has to be used in the most strategic and effective of ways. Their jobs are described by a series of 'competences' which may well inform how they are used, deployed and reviewed by their denomination. Congregations are 'judged' by their viability and there have to be special circumstances designed for small and ailing congregations to be maintained by the more vigorous ones. The world of support and development for clergy and for congregations is changing.

Baroness Perry has reviewed the Church of England's senior appointments processes and emphasizes that the strength of any revised appointments system will depend on the care and perceived fairness of the regular system of ministerial review, to which in theory all clergy are entitled. She says that a recorded process of review over a lifetime in ministry will give a fair and balanced account of a minister's vocation and its development. It will contain information about what resources have been invested in a minister's development along with information provided by a minister about their own strengths and weaknesses. Tellingly, she concludes that practice varies between denominations and dioceses and that not all ministers have the opportunity they deserve for an open assessment of leadership qualities among their many and varied talents and skills.

## Some ministerial outcomes

Led in this instance by the Church of England, the denominations are developing new ways in which to offer training programmes for ministers and lay people based on regional partnerships. These have the new title Regional Training Partnerships or RTPs. The 2006 report *Shaping the Future* describes the characteristics, associated with learning outcomes, which might be expected of ministers and those who provide their training.[2] I have adapted them slightly for ease of understanding and breadth of interpretation:

- To be able to speak of a sense of vocation to ministry and mission in ways which others have recognized which is obedient, realistic and informed;
- To be familiar with the traditions and practice of their denomination and to be able to represent the views of their denomination in public life;
- To show evidence of a spiritual discipline which will sustain and energize them in daily life;

- To be able to demonstrate a maturity of character having underlying strands which will sustain them under pressure and allow them to operate with integrity in flexible and balanced ways;
- To demonstrate self-awareness and self-acceptance as a basis for developing healthy professional and pastoral relationships;
- To be able to offer collaborative models of leadership in church and community in ways that demonstrate an example of faith and discipleship;
- To have a grasp of strategic issues and challenges within contemporary culture which will reflect a passion for mission to be expressed and communicated in appropriate ways.

This is a daunting list. Its only consolation is that it does point to Christ-like qualities. So that this new situation will not be perceived as terrifying in the extreme, denominations have developed considerable and sometimes impressive support systems. Clergy and congregations now have a range of specialist advisers who work alongside and who will accompany them into new patterns of working. Ministerial review and appraisal programmes are an expected part of the life of a diocese, district or province. I would want to encourage their use by ministers and congregations alike.

Many others use work consultants to help them keep their work in focus and maintain a work-life balance. The idea of consultancy, like some others with similar uses, needs to be unpacked in some detail. One important feature of consultancy is to ask questions about the direction of the organization. Ministerial review and work consultancy or coaching are set in the context of 'in order to do what?' Where do the tasks which are in any list fit into the overall aims of the organization? Review schemes first need to ask significant questions about the aims and goals of the organization and its leaders. In the past, many of those subjected to a barrage of review questions have wondered where the hidden message was about the overall aims of the church, diocese, district, bishop or chairman. Where the overall organizational aims are clear then there can be a harmony between the 'big picture' and the roles and responsibilities of each individual. Such transparency helps to keep us all 'on message'.

It is important to set out some basic understandings of review and external assessment in this section where we are exploring our knowledge of how well we are doing and how we can be accountable to others for what they expect us to do. These first comments and suggestions can apply as much to teams, groups, church councils or projects as to individuals. They all configure around words and ideas about consultancy which have come to be used and understood in very different ways, and often much too loosely.

## Work consultancy and mentoring

What then is consultancy? One of the most helpful developments of recent times is the use of an outside person or group who can work with the organization to gain an understanding of what is going on. Many groups will invite a person in to do a review of where they are. In the world-wide Church there was once a grand scheme across the Anglican Communion called *Partners in Mission* in which dioceses from different parts of the world would form an equal-partner relationship. With a growing sense of trust and understanding there could be an exchange of views and comment on how they saw and understood one another. That two-way collaboration has developed in a number of ways.

Many individuals use what is called a work consultant, whose task is different from that of a spiritual director. It involves an analysis of the work they are doing and the tasks they are expected to be involved with. Any good group or team will think it essential that they have an outside consultant if they are to be effective, professional and accountable.

Many things can go wrong with hiring a consultant. Perhaps it is best at this early stage for me to set out what the different terms might mean and what needs to be agreed when taking on a person or a group to do work of this kind.

The godfather of church-related consultancy work for me is the Revd Dr George Lovell, who has for many years developed sophisticated methods of analysing work situations. With Catherine Widdicombe he founded the training and consultancy agency *AVEC*. I was privileged to follow him as director for a few years. He has put together many of his ideas in a comprehensive book *Consultancy, Ministry and Mission*. His definition of consultancy work is this:

> Consultancy is a process of seeking, giving and receiving help aimed at aiding a person, group, church or organization to achieve their purposes in specific situations and circumstances. Analyses and designs are produced through the creative interplay between consultors and consultants as they focus on their work; the what and why and how of what they want to achieve in the circumstances in which they operate.[3]

## Some definitions

By way of introduction to consultancy I have scoured books and websites to gain some concise descriptions.

*Consultant* Someone or group completely independent of you or your organization who is asked to come in and listen, review and analyse your work or your organization and make suggestions or recommendations.

*Work consultancy* A process of thinking through issues with a trained person as they relate specifically to you and your work/ministry.

*Work consultant* A trained and experienced person who helps you to analyse, understand and develop the work which you have been asked to do.

*Organizational consultant* A trained and experienced person or group who are asked to analyse and make recommendations about your organization.

*Mentor* Someone with an understanding of your area of work or specialism who can accompany you through a task or series of tasks.

*Coach* Someone who can work with you to progress a task, understand a situation or help you to achieve objectives.

Some of these titles seem to be interchangeable in a rather loose way. That is why it is essential to know what you want when any one of these people or groups is hired. If there is a lack of clarity then you may feel deeply disappointed and the person asked to do the work let down and frustrated. An enormous amount of time can be wasted, money not well spent and, on occasions, a situation left worse than it was before.

## Basic approaches to consultancy

Trained consultants will have approaches which come from the way in which their own development has occurred. It will be important to explore these in an initial meeting. Some will have a pragmatic and practical approach drawn from years of experience in a particular area of work. Others will have as a part of their training group-analysis or psychological profile-skills. Whatever a consultant's background they will be bringing ideas and assumptions to bear on your situation and their analysis of it. You will be helped enormously if you can get those you are considering for your work to explain the approach they will be using. Some excellent people with great qualities and skills will fit what you are looking for while others with different approaches may not.

## Personal qualities to look for

- **Integrity** – if you feel that you cannot trust a person for any reason, not least in the area of confidentiality, then they are not to be used.
- **Reliability** – however good they are and have the skills you are looking for, if they cannot deliver what they promise then they cannot support you effectively.
- **Credibility** – will what a consultant says about themselves and the way they work persuade you, and others, to listen and respond to their interventions?

- **Technical expertise** – how is ability to do the job conveyed? Be suspicious if language used is so jargon-filled that you cannot understand what will happen.

## Basic questions

- Will they be doing the work themselves or will it be a colleague?
- What are the charges and what do they include?
- When do the charges begin?
- Where has work been done before and can other 'clients' be approached for a reference?
- How much time will be given and what level of service are you buying?
- If you are agreeing individual consultations, how frequently will they be, for how long will they last and over what period of time will they occur?
- If the commitment is ongoing, how and when will it be reviewed?
- What will happen to any written documentation?

## Criteria for success

The Acronym SMART is an easy way to examine whether the consultancy is what you want and comes from quarrying a helpful book by Anna Hipkiss, *Consultant, Be Your Best . . . and Beyond.*[4] You should ask whether the work is:

Specific
Measurable
Achievement focused
Realistic
Time bounded

## Questions to ask yourself

Before you, your team, your church council or whoever approaches a consultant, ask yourself these questions:

1 What is the objective?
2 When does the work need to be completed by?
3 What do you expect it to 'look' like when it is finished?
4 How will you know if the work has been successful?
5 What could go wrong?
6 Are there any charges above 'expenses'?
7 How do you want to feel when the work is completed?

## Essential ground rules for consultants

- Make a clear agreement before you begin.
- Build relationships at every contact level.
- Review and revise the agreement if any part of the situation changes.
- Identify lack of client commitment and act quickly.
- Keep reminding the client that an end has been agreed and that this gives a deadline for everyone to complete their work.
- Continue with your own professional development and in-service training.

One final comment which I always make to myself and frequently joke about to clients is: 'Remember they always have another meeting after you have gone!'

## What other people think about our work

Equally important as choosing a consultant is to ask what the outside world thinks of our work. There are a number of schemes which help to bring realistic feedback. We live in a world of opinion polls – politicians are told too frequently what their constituents and the wider public think of them. Focus groups are convened by marketing companies and media consultants to gain opinions from particular target groups. In this way instant feedback is acquired and products or behaviour refined. Yet there is a very real sense that these high-profile assessment methods are superficial. They are influenced by immediate mood or fashion and have an element of here today and forgotten tomorrow about them. Such indicators are not to be dismissed out of hand. They are helpful, and sometimes salutary, snapshots of opinion and of reaction to events and personalities who shape events and thought.

## 360° Review

More systematic and sensitive ways have been developed to help us understand what those around us think of our actions and activities. A particular method which has proved to be enormously helpful to clergy and to the activities of parish groups and leadership teams is called '360° review'. The use of a skilled consultant or trainer is essential. The programme has been taken from secular use, although it is 'new' for a description of church leadership because its use is only just coming into church life. It is an approach which can be of tremendous value, not only in the development of accurate self-knowledge, but also in the adaptation of approaches and work from an evidence-based type of feedback from those in the wider community. The Diocese of Oxford has created a programme called Developing Servant Leaders which uses this method. It has become so valued that some other dioceses and denominations have taken the method into their own review processes.

Because 360° review has to be accompanied by a skilled and trained person I am not going to give a full description here. As a general outline, what is offered is the opportunity to select a range of different people who encounter or experience your work or the work of your group. In a structured way they are asked to give views about your work in a range of areas. The trained consultant or facilitator will share this information with you or your group and will debrief those who took part in the review.

Work does not end with the results of 360° being shared. What will emerge is a range of issues for yourself and for those around you. Not everything will be pointing an accusing or an affirming finger at you! The person working with you will be able to see what has to be explored and will bring a range of resources into the process. Overall the work will take many months and will need revisiting regularly to ensure that the feedback has been really heard and that accompanied change is taking place.

A particularly good consequence of 360° review is that the views, hopes and expectations from those in the wider community can be brought in and matched with the hopes and expectations of those within. For churches and their staff this is a healthy way of allowing 'the kingdom' to break into otherwise closed systems. God can be seen and experienced beyond the ways in which the work of churches can be described. Outside voices can point to where God is at work outside the church and breathe fresh air into stagnating situations.

## Work is not everything

Although much of what we do in our work shapes who we are there is much more to life than work. A rounded or balanced life will very likely give a higher quality of performance at work not least because you will have a wider range of experiences to bring to whatever you are doing. A few people achieve more by an overwhelming focus on one thing and live exclusively for a cause. Many of these people take dramatic time off and do other equally concentrated or exciting things. Others focus enormously for a limited period of time and then suffer from burnout and may never fully recover.

What is new about leadership in this area is that very many programmes, courses and parts of the teaching in business schools and universities look at who we are as a person in the whole of life. There are many such programmes and I am describing one because it has caught my attention and encapsulates in a particularly engaging way what many do. It has been developed by the University of Liverpool Graduate into Employment Unit (GIEU) staff and is copyright restricted in the name of Dr Peter Hawkins and GIEU at Liverpool University (www. windmillsonline.co.uk). It is called the Windmills approach to Working, Learning, Playing and Giving and begins from this splendid quotation:

> 'When the wind blows, some people build walls – others build windmills'

This saying is based on the experience of its promoters that it is all too easy to build up barriers in life against change. We can become sophisticated in this without being aware of the destructive thing we are doing. Faced with overwhelming change in many aspects of their lives many people build walls to protect themselves. Equally, it is possible to see change as both challenging and liberating. When this approach is taken energy can be utilized in ways not unlike a windmill turning its sails into the wind. Here energy which drives sails turns the millstones or anything else which can be harnessed from the motion which is being created. To do this new kinds of thinking are needed and these begin with understanding where energy is created and harnessed in all of life.

In church terms a dramatic reversal of attitude would be needed. Denominations, like most historic organizations, change or adapt gradually. Many of their members and their leaders greet any proposal of change with a reference to things that have happened before rather than with a view of what might be created for the future. In one way that is right in so far as tradition can inform many debates and can certainly bring rich streams of spirituality into play to critique new and fashionable religious movements. There is a delicate balance, rarely achieved, between tradition and innovation. All too often the forces of conservatism, the wall builders, can pull change very closely back to holding the status quo.

There is also much experience of new ideas being pushed too fast and collapsing because there is not enough organizational support or the idea has not been thought through in ways that can anticipate over-exposure and exhaustion. Some of those appointed to innovative posts in denominations as a part of the Fresh Expressions ideas about faith sharing and church extension will testify to this.

The model that Windmills and many other schemes now use is one that will insist on a more rounded view of activities. Lifelong learning has been a part of the way in which adult theological education has been developed for many years now. Those who look at spirituality in work encourage us to see it as an integral part of the wholeness of life and not as a separate compartment. Four interlocking circles sum up very easily what experience now suggests. Religion is in danger of being trapped in the province of leisure time. The drawbacks of this are many and much work has been done to re-establish faith as an integral part of the whole of life. Giving comes with the application of faith and lives filled with service are seen as the essential outworking of faith. This is exemplified in the support for charities, schools and health care which is the traditional and well accepted province of Christian work.

It seems amazing to me that a secular programme, certainly with an enormous amount of humanity in it, can come up with a series of suggested themes which could equally well describe the Christian life. We would say that working, learning, playing and giving are essential ingredients in developing a whole life (Figure 11). Much of our spiritual direction and advice about formation has these ingredients.

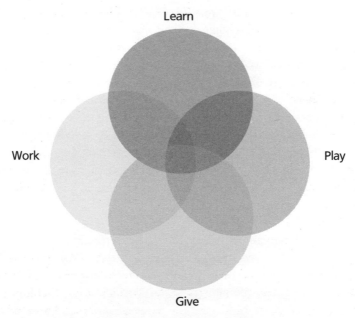

Figure 11: An integrated life

We need to use family, friends, spiritual directors, coaches and trainers, as well as those we work with to harness new ideas about how life is understood and developed. There is one final phrase which leaps out of the Windmills material for me:

> We spend more time planning our holidays than the rest of our lives

It is very true that one of the main times that families and friends talk to one another and make plans is before a holiday. Equally apparent is the absence of close family or friend conversations about goals and hopes in life and how these might be achieved. When things begin to go wrong it is too late for the right kind of conversation and there are no discussions or plans and dreams to draw upon.

## How are we doing as a congregation?

My work in conducting ministerial reviews when visiting clergy and parishes as an archdeacon and as a work consultant and mentor led me to construct what I thought was an accessible way of exploring the life of a congregation. The ideas had come to me first in another context as I was developing the Adult Catechumenate. They led me to look for certain features which are almost the DNA of a congregation. Without them an essential part of congregational life and development will be missing. These ideas are set out in more detail in a book I co-authored with Peter Ball called *Faith on the Way*.[5] I have since developed and refined them in many consultations and countless parish visitations. Since I was Archdeacon of Craven in the Diocese of Bradford for 11 years I have christened this new way of knowing how well a congregation is doing 'The Craven Grid' (Figure 12). I hope that those I worked with in the parishes will recognize a little of what I am now describing. Some might even attribute the development of their congregation to a close analysis of this kind!

**Figure 12: The Craven Grid: A template for parish life**

- **Welcome** simply means that there have to be many ways in which newcomers can be 'allowed' to enter into congregational life. The minister will establish an atmosphere of openness which will be experienced when newcomers enter a church or attend a social or teaching activity.
- **Deepening of faith** occurs when a congregation with its minister(s) pray and study together. A congregation which does not have a Lent or Advent course or Bible study notes and groups where faith is shared will not be deepening its own spirituality and will not be able to share its essential reason for existing.
- **Decision for commitment** will be demonstrated in the programmes or courses by which a congregation will introduce and initiate newcomers into the faith and life of that congregation and denomination.
- **Life in the church and in the world** will be experienced in the ways in which congregation members challenge the traditions and assumptions of their church and in how they draw energy from their common faith to live lives of service in the world.

## Will we ever know?

It is right that we will never know how well we are doing in a completely objective and fulfilling way. We do need to know what we are expected to do in our church roles, as ministers and as congregation and to be able to ask again what the Church is for. We do need to know what others think of us, as senior members of the denominations and as those who receive our work in our wider communities.

## What's new in denominational review?

A much needed and appropriate new world is emerging for ministers in relation to their denomination. Employment legislation protects those in conventional jobs. It is expected that there will be a job description and a person profile when a job is advertised. These are consolidated into a contract of appointment when a job is offered. Responsible employers will have in place an appraisal system, a complaints and grievance procedure and machinery for reviewing pay scales. Historically, little or none of this has been present in churches.

Most denominations have put in types of ministerial review and these have already been referred to. Coming alongside responsible review are clearer descriptions of what is expected of a minister, often now called 'competences'. When these are set out well in negotiation with a congregation and senior officers in a denomination an incoming minister will know what is expected. When an appointment is made a clear agreement at the outset gives something to measure against and evaluate should things go wrong. Without such mutually agreed areas of work and responsibility new developments and bright ideas brought in by the minister can easily descend into a series of mutual recriminations which are hard to disentangle.

What's new is that the terms on which a minister comes to an appointment are changing and are likely to change even more. The Church of England has appointed its ministers for centuries on a stipend, with accommodation, and a legal agreement which gives the person appointed security for life, or at least until retirement. Procedures to remove 'square peg' clergy are protracted and can be very expensive. Plans are well developed to move to a new way of making limited-term appointments. A new phrase, 'common tenure', is emerging to replace the age-old security of 'freehold'. Appointments are likely to be for a term of years with built-in reviews. Such reviews are likely to be separate from the pastoral support and visits which are given by bishops or archdeacons. Much has still to be worked out but the end result will mean that there should be much less uncertainty about knowing how well, or badly, a minister is doing.

Such agreements and reviews will bring significant changes to the relationship between a minister and their congregation. Those in free churches will be much more familiar with this situation, though not perhaps in such a structured way. One often stated unfortunate consequence has been the lack of freedom a minister has to lead or bring in changes and innovations. Such changes frequently alienate sections of a congregation and if they are influential groups this can lead to moves for the non-continuation of a minister's appointment. No one would want to reinforce such a situation. The active involvement of denominational officers and sometimes outside consultants is essential if ministers are to feel sufficiently secure and able to lead, with their teams, in a strategic way.

## A new form of security

Professionally structured review that arises from a well-planned appointments procedure is what should now be expected in any denomination. This is a considerable move forward from informal, and often impressionistic and sometimes unrealistic support and comment given to ministers by their superiors. Responsible review involves sections of the congregation and appropriate members of the wider community. It is beginning to model the open and collaborative style expected from clergy.

## WHAT'S NEW IN RECIPROCAL CARE?

Not to take steps to understand who we are and how well we are living out our Christian discipleship would be to live in an irresponsible way. Our faith by its very nature calls us on to new and exciting pathways of service. We need to be able to measure and strengthen the many ways in which we can respond to that call – minister, congregation and senior leaders together. Most of all we need to learn to care for ourselves. It is more than appropriate that this chapter should end with the four journeys of personal care which Professor Gillian Stamp commends to those who are leaders in any profession.[6]

All leaders know about burn-out – the time when we have given our all and can no longer be filled with creativity, bounce back and show optimism in the face of significant challenges. Leadership teams rise and fall and need renewing in many and creative ways. Gillian Stamp has been the friend and inspiration of very many senior church leaders and leadership teams. She has described what she calls *the four journeys* which all leaders and leadership teams need to make in order to continue to refresh themselves.

1 **The public journey** Here we put our knowledge and skills into places where practical leadership is exercised. In these places we are exposed to the full scrutiny of those we work with, and often of the general public. What we do is examined in critical ways by the external world and the assumptions of others. Leaders and leadership teams need to be secure in themselves and have a strong vision of where they are going. Such confidence is needed because many strategies have long time-scales. Such modern leadership, and certainly the leadership of parish clergy, will be of this kind in places where those who are experiencing or sharing in leadership may well have more expertise in their own area than their clergy. Such a journey of leadership needs deep inner resources.

2 **The private journey** This is the story of your life, or the life of the leadership group, which is shared with others. At a person-

al level it is the place where time is spent with family and friends or with leisure pursuits. For the team it is the time spent relaxing, eating together and mixing with groups in networks and those who see things in different ways. The private journey is your 'habitat'. It is all that belongs to the place you set out from and return to when you make your public journey.

3 *The personal journey* In this space we need to pause and explore who we are. It is the place to reflect on the pressures of the job and how they are changing us. It is a time for individuals to reflect on the integrity of the work which they are doing and, within that, the understandings of who they are becoming. Teams can become elite and exclusive, and certainly self-selecting. The personal journey is about self-knowledge and needs a skilled accompanier to help with profound explorations.

4 *The journey of the self* In this we blend together the experiences and skills which have formed us into the person we are or the group of which we are now part. In this is contained our academic skills, our knowledge base, which continues to grow and develop. Here is our experience, our knowledge of how we do things, sometimes called personal mastery. For leaders and leadership teams it is the experience we use to manage human situations. For those in exposed and responsible situations when they have to be the person or group to take an initiative it is 'what we do when we do not and cannot know what to do'. Here again is the test of characterfulness or 'default position' activities which are essential when trying to understand the pressures of leadership.

## Lead by example

To be seen to be caring for ourselves is certainly the best example to give to others. It shows we are committed to lifelong learning and personal development and we are not only giving the advice but taking it ourselves. Constant use of review and reflection is the only responsible way to give of our best and to make the most of the abilities, talents and responsibilities God gives to each one of us.

## Notes

1. See John Hull, 'Self-deception as a coping strategy for Christians', *Christian Action Journal*, Autumn 1995, pp. 19–21. Available from his website.
2. *Shaping the Future: New Patterns of Training for Lay and Ordained Ministers*, Church House Publishers, 2006.
3. George Lovell, *Consultancy, Ministry and Mission: A Handbook for Practitioners and Work Consultants in Christian Organizations*, Burns & Oates, 2000, p. 23.
4. Anna Hipkiss, *Consultant, Be Your Best . . . and Beyond*, Q Learning, Hodder & Stoughton, 2003.
5. Peter Ball and Malcolm Grundy, *Faith on the Way: A Practical Parish Guide to the Adult Catechumenate*, Continuum, 2000.
6. Gillian Stamp, *The Four Journeys*, available from Brunel Institute of Organisation and Social Studies, Brunel, The University of West London, Uxbridge, Middx UB8 3PH.

# What Could Be New in Leadership for the Future?

This has been a long journey and a great interweaving of example, story and theory. I have attempted to make a new offering of what I have experienced and discovered in the meanings of that many-faceted word 'leadership'. In Chapter 2 I highlighted a senior leader who based their work on a saying of Mahatma Gandhi, the leader who led by influence and example: 'The means are the ends in the making.' We now need to look at how the means of understanding leadership which I have described can be turned into ends as they come into the bloodstream of our congregations, local church groupings and denominations. When we look to the future and try to turn the dreams about what leadership could be like into a reality there are some clear steps that need to be taken. I am going to suggest that they can be divided into three sections; behaviour change, process change and hierarchical change. We can understand and influence the first two of these – and then hope and pray that the third will be an outcome!

Each of the chapters in this book has developed a facet of leadership from one angle or another. We now come to the point where a final chapter has to look at how the development of even better leaders can be achieved. You will not be surprised when I set out a collaborative solution. We have to look at how a culture of leadership development can become more firmly established. Can this central plank of support in each denomination become a fundamental part of the everyday work of all those who have present responsibilities in many different parts of our churches? I hope that those who are committed to a lifetime of work with local congregations will not think that I have deserted them in what I want to suggest, but that they and others will see the need for interconnectedness in all we do. How else should the Body of Christ be seen to work?

## BEHAVIOUR CHANGE

### The training and appointments divide

For a whole strand of church leaders to have collaborative team working as a basic method would be new. It would be even more innovative for there to be explanations, training programmes and support systems to hold this concept in place. What would also be new in a structural sense could be that denominations see an obvious link between leadership development and a necessary preparation for the appointment of their leaders, at whatever level. The connection between the support and development of leaders and placing them in the best possible appointments is fundamental to the quality of work in any organization. For each denomination the link between recruitment and training and the equipping of some ministers for senior appointments has to be explored in more depth because it is of such great importance and value.

It may by now be thought that anyone who has read to the last chapter of this book would be convinced of the need for systematic leadership development. Let me test your reactions.

- Should it not be the case that those who research into leadership have their findings taken up and used?
- Is it not the case that the parts of a denomination responsible for training see leadership development as an essential element in their work?
- Is it the case that those who support and make appointments in the denominations are closely linked with trainers and training organizations to identify and develop leaders for the future?

I do not yet experience a willingness across our denominations to give a wholehearted 'yes' to these questions.

## Formal and informal training

Let us start from where we are and see if my own conclusions are those which could attract debate, if not assent. There seem to be two ways in which leaders are developed and supported at the moment. One system is embedded within the official structures of a denomination and the other is developed by enthusiasts and interest groups whose concern is more for effective leadership training than for the making of the appointments themselves. I want to suggest a collaborative, co-operative, team-building solution which requires bringing both systems together in new and effective ways.

Even in denominations where senior leaders are elected, there is an obligation on present leaders and trainers to make sure that as wide a group as possible of able and equipped people are available for consideration and nomination. Baroness Pauline Perry says that since the publication of the first Report of the Committee on Standards in Public life (Chaired by Lord Nolan) public bodies and organizations have begun to be much more open and transparent in the way in which appointments are made.[1] She goes on to comment, citing the Church of England as an example, that at first there was not a willingness to join this openness. Her view is that since then attempts have been made to bring their appointments processes into line with best practice in the public sector. It is hoped that individuals will be able to put their name forward for any vacancy, and that they will be given an opportunity to correct any information made available to those making appointments.

# PROCESS CHANGE

## Investment in leadership

There are ways in which those committed to the training and development of leaders and those who help to make the appointments can make deliberate moves to bring about change and make their work more effective. The justification for this comes from my own personal experience. When I began my work as director of the Foundation for Church Leadership in March 2005 I was met with an avalanche of interest. Many people and organizations began to say that at last there is a Foundation which could co-ordinate thought and action in an impartial way. For most of my first year I tried to respond to this welcome by visiting or meeting as many as possible of those who were interested in the development of leadership in the churches. It began to become clear to me that my many stimulating encounters fell into four categories or types. I set these out in a 'mapping exercise' for my trustees and circulated a shorter document to many work colleagues. The four areas where I found a considerable interest in leadership are the places where I can see more co-operation leading to the provision of more effective leadership training.

In the months which followed I realized that these were not just four convenient subjects or activities for my own mind. They are four distinct areas of work or concern and without the contribution of any one of them there will not be a sustained and balanced development of leadership within the churches. The groupings are:

1  Those involved in research into leadership in universities and business schools;
2  The denominations who have leadership in their training programmes, both for initial and inservice training;
3  Organizations who lend themselves as a resource to the denominations to produce courses and networks concerned with leadership;
4  The wide range of people who offer their services to the denominations to act as coaches, mentors or consultants.

## Towards an ecology of sustainable leadership

I want to expand my descriptions of each area and suggest where the denominations and a network of colleagues might be able to concentrate their individual and collective energies so that leadership can become a key ingredient for the development of any local church or denomination. Here, there is a well-fitting parallel with our concerns for a sustainable environment. A balance of the elements and concerns about leadership such as I have been describing is necessary in order for a culture of leadership development to be recognized and sustained. There is a definite interconnectedness between informal systems and independent organizations and the official appointments systems of denominations. Many who become leaders in the denominations have been given their formation through involvement in independent training organizations and groupings. For some it has provided their principal means of inservice training. Like the desired ecological balance which is required to sustain life on our planet, in our particular area of concern there needs to be a deliberate attempt to create a sustainable balance between all the committed parties and groups so that a culture of leadership support and development can survive and flourish.

Each denomination, diocese, district or region has a significant group of officers who are responsible for designing and delivering the lay training and clergy inservice training needed for strategic leadership to be effective. Many important schemes have had lasting effect in some denominations. The current situation has been a good new development in that denominational training has the potential to be organized regionally in new collaborative groupings, the Regional Training Partnerships. These new organizations and their staff can only be effective if they are working closely with evidence-based information and some idea of the shapes of church which the present leadership is trying to develop. Some trainers and the courses and training they design will in themselves be a part of the leadership which is creating and reshaping the denominations collectively.

The separate groupings exist in an independent, unconnected way at the moment (Figure 13). My argument is to develop the idea of the need for a 'sustainable' ecology to the extent that suggestions for closer collaborations become natural and a necessity rather than an option to be worked at by those who have time and energy.

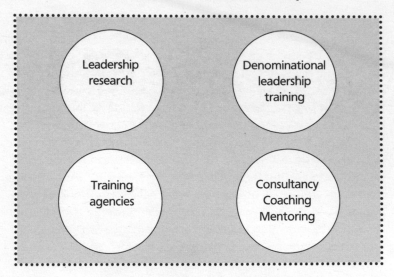

**Figure 13: Unconnected networks**

## Leadership research

Knowing what changes are taking place in our churches and the societies in which they are set is essential to any piece of strategic leadership. In commercial terms this is the research and development without which no new ideas or products can be created. There are colleagues in universities who have an interest in church organizations and leadership while others are interested in research on the psychology of religious organizations. Evidence-based research is a fundamental approach to developing the most appropriate training for leaders. The availability of research about what is happening in the wider world and among other world faiths is essential to decision-making and strategic planning within a denomination. It does not seem that the availability of information about social change and the changes within denominations has been taken up sufficiently when strategies are produced. 'Experience and intuition' appear to be main characteristics of leadership in some places while financial constraints have led policy decisions in others. There is a general feeling among researchers that church leaders are not willing to take too seriously the existing studies of organizations and changes in church life and attendance that have been thoroughly researched and painstakingly produced. The same could be said of research into teamwork and collaborative styles of leadership and of personality in ministry.

There is a basis for scepticism about evidence dictating decision-making. Strategic leaders have made reputations by taking decisions contrary to those suggested by facts presented to them, but only after a thorough reconnaissance of the territory. Unjustifiable these days is the disdain shown by some church leaders towards well-researched ideas about leadership, and what seems worse to some of them, management. Some of this mistrust stems both from an inherent distrust of the 'secular' gods of money, ambition and success and also from a mistrust of statistics. Some lay people have said to me about ideas I have brought about leadership and management into churches, 'we get enough of that at work'! Clergy and laity alike do not want that hostile world to creep into what they regard as the significantly different part of this, their religious or devotional life.

Alongside research institutions are those organizations and agencies which accompany people as they become better leaders and managers. The business schools have pioneered much research into leadership. Many among the staff have an interest in church leadership. As a contrast to this openness many church leaders mirror the response of senior managers and executives in being among those who are the lowest in a take-up of continuing training. Opportunities exist for those who are showing initial promise and who as leaders through their present work may well benefit from training alongside those in other professions at a similar stage in their careers.

What could be done:

- Research opportunities can and should be encouraged by directors of training in the denominations so that more clergy, perhaps at a mid-stage in their ministries, might begin study which draws on their experience and which enables them to know that the work they are doing is valued.

- Church leaders could be encouraged more confidently to take into account evidence about change which is taking place in the area in which they are responsible.
- Training opportunities offered by universities and business schools could be investigated more thoroughly and offered more widely to leaders and leadership teams.

## Denominational leadership training

Each denomination, diocese, district or region has a significant group of officers who are responsible for designing and delivering the lay training and clergy inservice training needed for strategic leadership to be effective. Many important schemes have had lasting effect in some denominations. The new Regional Training Partnerships now offer a new opportunity for denominational training. These groupings are slowly emerging after a thorough look at the ecumenical possibilities in newly suggested regions for both initial and inservice training. The new partnership agencies are also likely to offer significant training for lay people from local churches, many of whom are in significant leadership roles. Their staff can only be effective if they are working closely with evidence-based information and some idea of the shape of church which the present leadership is trying to develop. Some trainers and the course content they develop will in themselves be a part of the leadership which is creating and reshaping the church.

Almost every leader I meet and every article I read about leadership emphasizes the importance of putting together an effective team. Church life is unusual in that many senior leadership groups are put together by nomination from a number of different routes and not always as a result of the choice or active participation of the team leader. This places a particular challenge on those who are appointed to enable the team to be effective in their work. The need for team-building support is more pressing than ever.

Added to this challenge is the need to develop strategies which will command sufficient support among the members of congregations and their clergy for change to take place. Strategic team leadership is an important modern concept. It challenges the strong personality and party differences which exist in many senior ecclesiastical teams. The evolution of how churches have learned to adapt and survive would make an interesting study in itself.

What could be done:

- More thought could be given by those who make senior appointments about the nature of the teams they are appointing staff to join or to lead.
- Team leaders need support and sometimes consultancy to assist them in building their diverse members into teams. The systematic provision of this could be developed by a partnership between official and external agencies.
- Once established, senior teams should take, as one of their principal tasks, the development of strategies which will enable congregations and clergy to feel that there is a sense of overall direction in their work.
- Regional Training Partnerships need to include an element of leadership training for clergy and lay people in their new programmes wherever possible.

## *Training agencies*

We have already seen in Chapter 7 that change in the denominations has been brought about as much by leadership from the edges as by central initiatives and policies. Through deliberate attempts at collaboration there is now an informal network of agencies across Britain which constitutes a significant training resource. Some of these deliver training while others form interest networks and produce consultations, lectures and publications. Important for the future is that many of these organizations are led and staffed by lay persons, who can bring considerable expertise from the secular world. What they also offer is a systematic and professional approach to the development of leadership.

Suggested actions:

- The network of agencies should be strengthened and appropriate new members brought in.
- Those agencies that deliver training should be supported and their provision promoted in association with academic training providers and the Regional Training Partnerships.

## Consultants, coaches and mentors

Leaders need to be supported and accompanied in their work. Leadership teams cannot function in creative ways without external facilitation. If they think they can then either there is a lack of confidence about allowing someone from outside to see what they are really like or there is a lack of objectivity and no one to hold the team to agreed goals. I have encountered a significant number of impressive people and organizations who offer consultancy, coaching and mentoring of one kind or another. Some are trained and supported by church networks, others have professional qualifications while yet others work on reputation and previous experience of leadership.

There remain some structures to be put in place for those who could give even more support to church leaders in these ways. Some of those from the secular world who are engaged as consultants to leaders and teams get overcome either by the complexity of church life or are over-impressed by the ecclesiastical culture and ambience within which church leaders operate. There needs to be developed a 'module' which introduces external consultants to the ways in which denominations work. This would assist them in their objectivity, allow them to ask the right questions before they agree to take on work and avoid unfortunate and unhappy misunderstandings. There is a significant piece of work ahead for all of us, or for one group on behalf of the rest, to develop criteria for those offering their services to church leaders and leadership teams.

Suggested actions:

- Some work should be done to co-ordinate consultancy networks and people.

- A set of objective criteria should be established for those who work with leaders and leadership teams and for those who consider hiring them.
- A process of induction should be established for those who offer consultancy or mentoring to leaders and leadership teams within the denominations.

## *Voluntary co-ordination*

A half-way house for bringing together those concerned with leadership would be voluntary co-operation (Figure 14). The interested parties could opt to exchange information, databases and website links. This would provide a significant resource for those who wanted to find out more about consultancy for church leaders and where to go for training and support. It misses out the important element of involvement by national denominational ministerial development departments and also the appointments systems for any denomination. It is a significant place to begin and I am very pleased that some energy is already being expended to bring these groupings together.

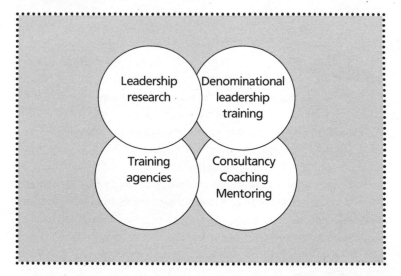

Figure 14: Networks in a voluntary grouping

## Leadership collaboration

The type of collaboration described in the previous section leaves one question unanswered. How are those concerned with making appointments from within the denominations to make best use of external resources? There is still a temptation to regard the groups I have described above as external to the appointments process and thus not major contributors to the support and development of leaders in any denomination. The separation can be described by adding another circle to my initial diagram (Figure 15).

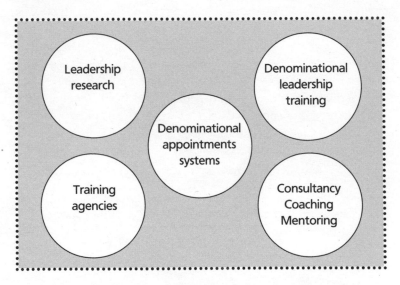

**Figure 15: A disconnected appointments system**

Such a compartmentalizing of activities benefits no one except those who gain by keeping the organizations and groupings separate. The biggest disadvantage is that it continues to contribute to caricature and misunderstanding. From the arguments I have set out it seems self-evident for the barriers between officialdom and voluntary partnership to be further broken down. A new richness would develop which would not only be a benefit to all but would also reflect the actual nature of churches as open organizations where there is a great mixture of innovation from many places and the necessary professional standards and safeguards which any responsible organization should have in place. A newly developed and mature partnership might look much more like that described in the diagram below (Figure 16).

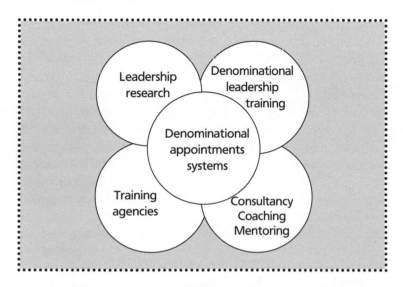

Figure 16: Integrated networks linked to appointments

## A new win-win ministerial partnership

If what could be added to such descriptions was the inclusion of the leadership training and best practice in appointments procedures from the voluntary and public sectors there might be one significant and important extra new development – and possibly the most important for the future – that boundaries are crossed and that leadership training within the churches steps on to a wider stage. Those currently in ministerial leadership positions within the denominations would feel more within themselves that they are being supported and that there is a comprehensive programme of development for them. A consequence of this is that some of those considering a call to ministry might see a present leadership which was making deliberate attempts to renew itself.

## HIERARCHICAL CHANGE

### The call to new work

Of direct relevance to joining up the training and appointments systems in the denominations is the acceptance of the concept that vocation is not a once-for-all thing. Dangerous in the extreme is the belief that the content of an initial calling to Christian ministry, or to any other work, will remain essentially the same throughout a working lifetime. The basic idea that we grow and develop is one essential part of the renewing of vocation. The other part is the realization that work changes and develops and that its demands differ as our time in particular posts goes on. It is essential to understand that we are in particular pieces of work for a time only. The development of vocation means that we can be called on to do new things both by God and by the attraction and demands of new work.

The individualism which surrounds the work of a minister or senior church leader appears to have as one of its consequences that there are few resources available to assist a person in their own thinking about when it is appropriate to move on from one post to another. The secrecy which surrounds the consideration of appointments in some denominations colludes with an absence of 'career' support and guidance.

Here in a most important way is the place where a work consultant can be of support alongside the formal process of ministerial review. It is impossible for a person on their own, or in conversation with immediate colleagues or close family, to decide when it is right to move on – or what the possibilities of new work are. Just as significant is the difficulty of local consultation about moving on. First of all there is the problem of even suggesting to congregation members that a move for their minister is being considered. Second there is a sense of impossibility about getting objective advice from congregational sources. It is just the wrong place to ask such questions. Here again, there is an immediate need for denominational review processes and independent support and consulting agencies to be able to offer positive and realistic advice at key transition points in ministerial and congregational life. Engaging such joined-up combined resources needs to be part of the fundamental core belief that new situations require new responses and that a call to new work needs preparation and appropriate training.

## Non-hierarchical development

What would be very new in the development of leadership within any organization would be a two-way mobility. In some of the historic free churches there is perhaps a greater tendency than in episcopally led denominations for senior people to return to local appointments. When I worked as a chaplain within the National Coal Board many years ago I encountered a programme where miners who could no longer cope with the physical demands of work underground were not superannuated to 'light duties' on the surface. They were appointed as 'parent craftsmen' to those who were preparing for the hazardous and demanding work of mining coal at the many new faces which were then being opened up. In this way there was a genuine recognition that skills learned at one stage in life were still of value and could be shared in important new ways without loss of face or pride.

Interesting indeed would be the development of a programme where leaders and those who had been in sole charge of congregations for years moved into specialist team membership positions. Our churches are still places where many people, especially senior leaders, will be in place for ten or many more years. A way of developing methods of sharing expertise and of valuing skills without remaining in one post for too long would be revolutionary. In practice, there might well be the need to address differentials in pay and support at the same time. There would also need to be support and advice for some partners who had shared a busy life at senior level to enable them to adjust to a change in status.

How to leave, and to leave well, is a skill in itself. The move to new work which was accompanied by a searching review of a person's present skills and the needs of a denomination could make any move much better understood by all involved. The sense that a living vocation is still being addressed is very important indeed. A call to new work is also a call to understand how God goes before us and which leadership skills can be contributed and which will need to be put in place for the next phase of a working life.

## A new profile for leaders

Joined-up thinking and activity about developing and supporting leaders would not only benefit those who are struggling to survive with the pressures of work in the denominations today. It would also give important messages to those who might consider offering themselves for ministerial work in the future. Stated in a negative way, the decline in numbers of those coming into ministry could be accounted for by present perceptions of the work. One of these is that the picture of a minister, or senior leader, in any denomination today is one of significant overwork and stress. Those who look towards ministry inside the churches do not always see the most attractive of pictures.

A denomination, or a grouping of denominations, which took the support and development of its personnel seriously could well become one that attracted more able people to come and work in it. Failure to bring together leadership training and progress through an organization will produce dysfunctional leaders. If a denomination has a culture of individualism, and of competitiveness, then it will attract the kind of personality who thrives in such an atmosphere. The profile of denominational leadership for the future, alongside desired patterns of leadership in other places, will not be of this kind. Collaborative teamwork will be a norm. A separation of this fundamental working methodology from the way in which development through a denomination is carried out will give the message that engagement in collaborative training will weaken or frustrate promotion prospects. The profile of leadership for the future will be effective, and attract an appropriate kind of person, only if it demonstrates a clear and public connection between training and support in particular kinds of leadership and the appointments which a denomination makes.

## Leadership and evangelism

The purpose of developing leadership in a church is not for there to be effective ways to keep going in much the same way as today. Leadership development goes alongside an understanding of how the strategy and purposes of a denomination can best be developed. A central and key part of this type of leadership is that it works to share the aims of the denomination in as wide a way as possible and then brings in leaders who can share faith and extend membership.

There are many exciting challenges ahead. One of them is developing new ways of bringing faith to young people and to young adults. The support and development of leaders in the Fresh Expressions and New Shapes of Church movements is essential for this. There is also the need to affirm and develop those types of leadership which will attract and keep the faithful regulars and elderly within the denominations. As specialized targeting of groups within the population becomes more sophisticated there is also the need for those who keep mainstream or minority congregations going to feel affirmed and supported. New members do not join groups where the atmosphere is bad and whose members and ministers feel deserted or unaffirmed by their denomination.

More than anything else evangelism unites because it gives a clear definite objective – to know Christ and to make him known. It needs to unite because it gives a shared sense of excitement about the reason for there being a congregation, denomination or church at all. An evangelism that divides defeats the object of the faith-sharing exercise. Rival groupings about language in the expression of faith or styles of ministry contribute to the development of sectarian and exclusive expressions of belief. These divisions, experienced all over the world, can only be combated by those in leadership at many levels having a broader picture of what a faithful and faith-filled community can achieve.

A leadership which unites can see that many styles and types of language and liturgy are needed within one comprehensive organization if many levels of communication and evangelism are to be effective. Leadership training and development which begins at the stage of initial recruitment and ends with senior appointments will be designed to give this.

We do not know what shapes the church of the future will have. We can be excited by the invitation to lead and to explore and to begin to create them. The God who has called us to particular pieces of work at one stage in life is a God who is faithful. There will be further calls and new work. The continuing refreshment of our spiritual life will give us ears to hear that call and the eyes of faith to see the next steps in our journey. We are rarely, if ever, called to that new work on our own. New partnerships will show us that there are many ways in which the world can help make leadership more effective within our churches. Our response is to be with colleagues and believers who have grasped a new vision for leadership. They are excited by a desire to share their faith and invite us to travel with them. To respond to the call to leadership is in itself an act of faith.

## Notes

1. See her chapter, 'Lessons from the secular world' in the collection of essays edited by John Adair and John Nelson, *Creative Church Leadership*, Canterbury Press, 2004, pp. 114–15.

# Contact Organizations and Websites

## Networking organizations with a leadership focus

**Alban Institute,** 7315 Wisconsin Ave, Suite 1250W, Bethesda, MD, 20814–3211, USA. www.alban.org

**CABE (Christian Association of Business Executives)** is a network of Christians in business life who share common concerns and who seek to promote the application of business principles in the working environment: www.cabe-online.org

**CHRISM** is a cross-denominational association for Ministers in Secular Employment and offers support for ordained and lay people in the workplace: www.chrism.org.uk

**Christian Research,** Vision Building, 4 Footscray Road, Eltham, London SE9 2TZ. 020 8294 1989, admin@christian-research.org.uk, www.christian-research.org.uk

**Common Purpose:** A networking, development and training organization that works with civil society, faith, business and political leaders: www.commonpurpose.org.uk

**CPAS (Church Pastoral Aid Society)** Arrow Leadership Programme, Athena Drive, Tachbrook park, Warwick CV34 6NG: www.cpas.org.uk

**Foundation for Church Leadership** is a networking, database and research agency which aims to support, encourage and inspire church leaders: www.churchleadershipfoundation.org

**Heythrop Institute for Religion, Ethics and Public Life** is a centre for research and reflection on contemporary issues including work and leadership: www.heythrop.ac.uk/HIREPL

ICF (Industrial Christian Fellowship) is an ecumenical organization which acts as a challenging resource for churches to understand the world of work and a support for Christians in the workplace: www. icf-online.org

IMA (Industrial Mission Association) is the professional association of industrial chaplains and their associates: Secretary, Andy Smith at asmith@fish.co.uk

LICC (London Institute for Contemporary Christianity) works to engage Christians as they engage biblically and relevantly with the issues they face including those of leadership and work: www.licc.org.uk

MODEM (Managerial and Organisational Disciplines for the Enhancement of Ministry) is an ecumenical Christian network which seeks to initiate dialogue between exponents of leadership, organization, spirituality and ministry: www.modem.uk.com

Ridley Hall Foundation is the long-term project at Ridley Hall Theological College, Cambridge which is concerned with relating Christian faith to the business world: www.ridley.cam.ac.uk

St Paul's (Cathedral) Institute was founded in 2002 to create a forum for reflection, open debate, education and action on the spiritual and ethical issues facing business: www.stpauls.co.uk

## Contacts with those who offer leadership training opportunities

Details of what each organization offers can be obtained from their website

Grubb Institute, Cloudesley Street, London N1 oHU. 020 7278 8061. ebl@grubb.org.uk, www.grubb.org.uk

Telos Partners, Gainsborough House, 59–60 Thames Street, Windsor, Berks SL4 1TX. 01753 833377. info@telospartners.com, www. telospartners.com

St Deiniol's Library: Church Lane, Hawarden, Flintshire CH5 3DF. 01244 532350. deiniol.visitors@btconnect.com, www.st-deiniols.org

St George's House: Windsor Castle, Berks SL4 1NJ. 01753 848848. stgeorges.house@ukonline.co.uk, www.stgeorgeshouse.org

## Contact Organizations and Websites

**The Leadership Institute:** Tli Office, Hilgay Rectory, Church Road, Hilgay, Downham Market, Cambs PE38 0JL. 01366 382969. TLIoffice@aol.com, www.tli.org.uk

**The Leadership Trust:** Weston-under-Penyard, Ross-on-Wye, Herefordshire HR9 7YH. 01989 767667, enquiries@leadership.org.uk, www.leadership.org.uk

**The Windsor Leadership Trust:** Gainsborough House, 59–60 Thames Street, Windsor, Berks SL4 1TX. 01753 272050. office@windsorleadershiptrust.org.uk, www.windsorleadershiptrust.org.uk

# Bibliography

Adair, John, *How to Find your Vocation: A Guide to Discovering the Work You Love*, London, Canterbury Press, 2000.

Adair, John, *Effective Strategic Leadership*, London, Pan Books, 2003.

Adair, John and Nelson, John, *Creative Church Leadership*, London, Canterbury Press, 2004.

Adie, Michael, *Held Together: An Exploration of Coherence*, London, DLT, 1997.

Arbuckle, Gerald A., *Refounding the Church: Dissent for Leadership*, London, Cassell (Geoffrey Chapman), 1993.

Avis, Paul, *Authority, Leadership and Conflict in the Church*, London, Cassell (Mowbray), 1992.

Ball, Peter and Grundy, Malcolm, *Faith on the Way*, London, Continuum, 2000.

Bayes, Paul and Sledge, Tim, *Mission-shaped Parish*, London, Church House Publishing, 2006.

Becker, Penny Edgel, *Congregations in Conflict: Cultural Models of Local Religious Life*, Cambridge, 1999.

Berger, Peter, *The Social Reality of Religion*, London, Faber & Faber, 1969, Penguin University Books, 1973.

Carr, Wesley, *The Priestlike Task: A Model for Training and Developing the Church's Ministry*, London, SPCK, 1985.

Clark, David (ed.), *Changing World, Unchanging Church? An Agenda for Christians in Public Life*, London, Cassell (Mowbray), 1997.

Clements, Keith, *Lovers of Discord, Twentieth Century Theological Controversies in England*, London, SPCK, 1988.

Craig, Yvonne, *Learning for Life: A Handbook of Adult Religious Education*, London, Cassell (Mowbray), 1994.

Croft, Steve, *Ministry in Three Dimensions*, DLT, 1999.

Croft, Steve (ed.), *The Future of the Parish System*, Church House Publishing, 2006.

Downs, Thomas, *The Parish as a Learning Community, Modeling for Parish and Adult Growth*, New York, Toronto, Paulist Press, 1979.

# Bibliography

Drucker, Peter, *The Age of Discontinuity: Guidelines to Our Changing Society*, London, Pan Books, 1968.

Duffy, Eamon, *The Voices of Morebath, Reformation and Rebellion in an English Village*, New Haven and London, Yale University Press, 2001.

Dulles, Avery, *Models of the Church: A Critical Assessment of the Church in All its Aspects*, Dublin, Gill & Macmillan, revised edition, 1987.

Ecclestone, Giles (ed.), *The Parish Church: Explorations in the Relationship of the Church and the World*, London, Mowbray/The Grubb Institute, 1988.

Francis, Leslie and Robbins, Mandy, *Personality and the Practice of Ministry*, London, Grove Books, Pastoral Series P9, 2004.

Freire, Paulo, *Pedagogy of the Oppressed*, London, Sheed & Ward, 1972, Penguin Books, 1972.

General Synod of the C of E, *Breaking New Ground: Church Planting in the Church of England*, London, Church House Publishing, 1994.

Gilbert, Peter, *Leadership, Being Effective and Remaining Human*, London, Russell House Publishing, 2005.

Green, Laurie, *Let's do Theology: A Pastoral Cycle Resource Book*, London, Cassell (Mowbray), 1990.

Greenwood, Robin, *Transforming Priesthood: A New Theology of Mission and Ministry*, London, SPCK, 1994.

Greenwood, Robin, *Practising Community: The Task of the Local Church*, London, SPCK, 1996.

Greenwood, Robin and Burgess, Hugh, *Power, Changing Society and the Churches*, London, SPCK, 2005.

Grundy, Malcolm, *An Unholy Conspiracy: The Scandal of the Separation of Church and Industry since the Reformation*, Canterbury Press, 1992.

Grundy, Malcolm, *Community Work*, Cassell Mowbray, 1994.

Grundy, Malcolm, *Understanding Congregations*, Cassell Mowbray, 1998. (out of print)

Grundy, Malcolm, *What They Don't Teach You at Theological College*, Canterbury Press, 2003.

Handy, Charles, *Understanding Organisations*, London, Penguin Books, 4th edn, 1993.

Handy, Charles, *The Empty Raincoat: Making Sense of the Future*, London, Hutchinson, 1994.

Harvey-Jones, John, *Making it Happen: Reflections on Leadership*, London, Collins, 1988.

Hastings, Adrian, *The Shaping of Prophecy: Passion, Perception and Practicality,* London, Cassell (Geoffrey Chapman), 1995.

Higginson, Richard, *Transforming Leadership: A Christian Approach to Management*, London, SPCK, 1996.

Hipkiss, Anna, *Consultant, Be Your Best and Beyond*, London, Hodder & Stoughton, Q Learning, 2004.

Howard, Sue and Welbourne, David, *The Spirit at Work Phenomenon*, Azure, 2004.

Hudson, Mike, *Managing without Profit: The Art of Managing Third-sector Organisations*, London, Penguin Books, 1995.

Hull, John, *Mission-Shaped Church: A Theological Response*, SCM Press, 2006.

Hybells, Bill, *Courageous Leadership: Stories from Willow Creek*, Zondervan, Grand Rapids, Michigan 49530, 2002.

Lovell, George, *Analysis and Design*, London, Burns & Oates 1994.

Lovell, George, *Consultancy, Ministry and Mission*, London, Burns and Oates, 2000.

Lovell, George and Widdicombe, Catherine, *Churches and Communities: An Approach to Development in the Local Church*, London, Search Press, 1978 and 1986.

Martineau, Jeremy, *The Vicar Is Leaving*, Arthur Rank Centre, 1998.

Morisy, Ann, *Beyond the Good Samaritan: Community Ministry and Mission*, London, Cassell/Mowbray, 1997.

Nelson, John (ed.), *Managing and Leading: Challenging Questions for the Churches*, London, Canterbury Press for MODEM, 1988.

Nelson, John (ed.), *Management and Ministry: Appreciating Contemporary Issues*, London, Canterbury Press for MODEM, 1996.

Patel, Ketan J., *The Master Strategist: Power, Purpose and Principle*, Hutchinson, 2005.

Pattinson, Stephen, *The Faith of the Managers: When Management becomes Religion*, London, Cassell, 1997.

Percy, Martin and Turnbull, Richard (eds), *Leadership in Mission Shaped Churches: Emerging Theological and Practical Models*, Canterbury Press, to be published in 2007.

Peters, Thomas J., *Liberation Management: Necessary Disorganization for the Nanosecond Nineties*, New York, Alfred A Knopf, 1992.

Peters, Thomas J. and Waterman, Robert H., *In Search of Excellence: Lessons from America's Best-run Companies*, New York, Harper & Row, 1982.

Platten, James and Chandler, Andrew (eds), *New Soundings: Essays on Developing Tradition*, London, DLT, 1996.

Reed, Bruce, *The Dynamics of Religion: Process and Movement in Christian Churches*, London, DLT, 1978.

Reeves, Donald, *Down to Earth: A New Vision for the Church*, Cassell (Mowbray), 1997.

# Bibliography

Rudge, Peter, *Order and Disorder in Organisations*, Australia for CORAT, 1990.

Schillebeeckx, Edward, *Ministry: A Case for Change*, London, SCM Press, 1981.

Senge, Peter, *The Fifth Disciplines: The Art and Practice of the Learning Organisation*, London, Random House, Doubleday, 1999.

Shaw, Peter, *Mirroring Jesus as Leader*, Grove Books Ethics Series E135, 2004.

Sykes, Stephen, *Power and Christian Theology*, Continuum, 2006.

Wagner, C. Peter, *Leading your Church to Growth*, London, MARC Europe, 1984.

Warren, Robert, *Building Missionary Congregations*, London, Church House Publishing, 1995.

Watts, Fraser, Nye, Rebecca and Savage, Sarah, *Psychology for Christian Ministry*, Routledge, 2002.

# Index